Thank you – that's all we need for today . . .

A Practical Guide to Musical Theatre Auditions

Mary Hammond

with Emer Gillespie

and Nigel Lilley

Peters Edition Limited
2–6 Baches Street
London N1 6DN

Tel: 020 7553 4000
Fax: 020 7490 4921
email: sales@editionpeters.com
internet: www.editionpeters.com

ISBN 978-1-84367-030-8

A catalogue record for this book is available from the British Library

CD recorded at The Bakery. Engineer: Rik Simpson. Vocalists: Mary Hammond and Adam Linstead. Pianist: Stuart Morley.

Cover design by Adam Hay. Cover photograph by Adam Wright.

Printed in England by Halstan & Co, Amersham, Bucks.

Putting a show together is like a jigsaw puzzle. This means that there is a mental picture of a show and the casting director will be working on it piece by piece. Each piece of the puzzle will be determined by those already in place.

David Grindrod (casting director)

I like people who are prepared to take a risk with material. It is important for a director to see a creative artist.

Trevor Jackson (casting director)

Too often in auditions, candidates for roles sing sans point of view. It is imperative for me that singing actors have a handle on what it is they're singing about and be able to make thought-processes manifest in performance. Think, think, think. Under-preparation is also a bug-bear of mine – it's nothing less than bone idleness.

Gareth Valentine (musical director)

Real talent isn't always immediately classifiable. It can't be defined by whether or not you get a job.

Matt Ryan (director)

Contents

Introduction

Over the past 25 years, there has been a considerable change in the training of musical theatre in Britain. I have been lucky enough to be part of the development of the industry that makes it what it is today. When I first started coaching, it was accepted that dancers were sent to auditions and only required to sing "Happy birthday to you" in different keys and "Somewhere over the rainbow" (a subtle test of that octave leap). Now there are many highly-skilled performers competing for parts, and the ability to show your individuality and skill in an audition is a vital requirement.

To show who you are and what you can do in the space of a few minutes can feel like a daunting task. As a singing teacher and vocal coach, I have spent a considerable amount of time both preparing performers for different kinds of auditions and sitting on panels watching them cope with this most unnatural of situations. In my experience, it is mostly fear of the unknown which stops people showing themselves at their best. In writing this book, I've tried to think of all the things that I didn't know when I started out, and to suggest a practical approach to showing yourself at your best.

Over the years, many of my students have asked me: "How can I stop being nervous?" My answer – probably gratingly simple – is: "Know what you are doing." Or, as Anne McNulty, casting director for the Donmar Warehouse, says: "Preparation, preparation, preparation." Most auditions take place at short notice, but it should be possible to assess what the casting director/creative team might be looking for, and then to choose suitable material and show the necessary qualities in the audition room. While this publication stops short of being a "how-to-sing" book, I will talk about the importance of using a variety of vocal styles to suit the material you are singing, as well as encouraging close reading of the lyrics.

Although principally geared towards performers hoping to work in a professional capacity, this book is equally useful for the many people who work in youth theatre and amateur dramatic societies. In fact, these companies often provide a key way of gaining performing experience for anyone entering the profession.

I hope that the checklist on page 102 is useful not only to those starting out, but also to those who are more experienced – it is useful to have something to jog your memory and give a structure to your audition day. The first time I learnt this was many years ago when a student of mine said that he had an audition at 9.30am and couldn't possibly be at his best so early as he was used to going to bed at 1am! Remembering that it took me five years to get used to getting up early when I had kids, I tried to be sympathetic. I suggested he put his alarm on at 6.30am, did half an hour of physical exercises, ate a really good breakfast, did some vocal warm-ups (a ten-minute tape I'd recorded for him), got washed, dressed and left lots of time to get to the venue. I said you'll probably feel terrible by midday, but you will have done a good audition. I felt quite strange saying all this the first time – I was quite young and felt unnecessarily bossy dictating his timetable. But he said he had found that it really worked.

This all seems entirely natural to me now. I've had years of studying voice science and am now considerably more informed. However, much of the advice contained in this book is based on common sense. Although it is supported by knowledge, most practical things are obvious – once you know what they are! So let's take the mystery out of auditioning and help show who you are and what you can do.

Mary Hammond

Acknowledgements

It would not have been possible for me to assemble my thoughts into any sort of order without discussions with, and help from, so many people actively engaged in the process of auditioning. These include Jill Green, David Grindrod, Trevor Jackson, Anne McNulty, Stephen Mear, Matt Ryan, Gareth Valentine, Alex Worrall and my colleagues at the Royal Academy of Music.

I have also been fortunate to sit on panels with and to be part of a process that involves inspiring directors and musical directors – thanks to all of them.

I am very grateful to the eight musical theatre artistes who agreed to be interviewed about their experiences and whose insights give such real-life context to the book.

I would like to thank Adam and Stuart for their work on the recording, for the engineer Rik, and Coldplay for the use of their studio. Thanks also to Andrew Hanley at Peters Edition for his patience and guidance.

Importantly, I would certainly never have had the skill to transfer my thoughts into book form without help from Nigel Lilley and Emer Gillespie – eternal gratitude.

Finally, a note of thanks to my family for their tolerance of my despair at ever finding time to finish this book!

The aims of this book

This book answers a number of important questions:

- What is an audition and how do you get one?
- Is it best to go through an agent? Can you get an audition independently or go to an open audition?
- How do you choose a suitable song? How do you make the best vocal and acting choices when presenting it?
- Have you prepared your song thoroughly and does it allow your individuality to shine through?
- What is the best way of making sure you are both vocally and physically in good shape for the audition?
- The audition panel: who are you likely to meet and what are their jobs?
- How should you present yourself during the audition?
- Coping strategies: what are the best things to do before, during and after the audition?

What is an audition?

*An audition can be daunting but try and remember that it's
essentially an arena in which to express your talent.*

Matt Ryan (director)

An audition is your chance to show your ability as a performer
and an opportunity to show your individuality to a panel of
prospective employers. The audition may involve singing,
acting or dancing, depending on the project. The best way
to approach it is with a positive attitude, embracing the
opportunity to perform. Remember the pleasure of playing
to an audience – and why you embarked on this career in the
first place.

An auditionee should aim to project to a panel:

- I hope you want to work with me.
- I hope I want to work with you.

The process

A production company embarking on a new project, or
recasting an existing one, will usually ask a casting agent to
find suitable artists for it to choose from. After discussions with
the creative team, the casting agent will produce a breakdown
of parts to be sent out to agents. This can have details of roles,
characters, vocal range and style, suggested playing age,
possible colouring and physical type.

Once this has been issued to the agents, it is their job – and
skill – to look at their client-list and select suitable artists to
put forward.

Casting breakdowns

Here are some examples of casting breakdowns:

MAMMA MIA!

ALL ARTISTS TO HAVE STRONG POP/ROCK SOUND AND BE ABLE TO MOVE WELL.

ROSIE: Late 30s. One of Donna's oldest friends. Was a former singer with "Donna & the Dynamos". Sophisticated, sharp-tongued and elegant. Featured role. Vocal range: strong belt with good range.

ALI: Early 20s. Sophie's friend. Character girl. Has a healthy cynicism about men! Featured role. Vocal range: strong belt, good soprano an advantage.

SAM: Around 40. May be Sophie's father. Left Donna because of an obligation to his fiancé. Became an architect. He's a charmer. Featured role. Vocal range: tenor

SKY: Late 20s. Sophie's fiancé. He's athletic, attractive, sensitive and self-aware. Formerly worked at the London Stock Exchange – has a passion for the island and the people. Featured role. Vocal range: baritone/tenor.

And here is a casting breakdown from the Donmar Warehouse's production of *Merrily We Roll Along*.

MERRILY WE ROLL ALONG

FRANKLIN SHEPHERD: A composer – latterly a music then a film producer. A member of the trio of friends. Graduated from Lake Forest Academy with Charley and Mary in 1965. Has composed three musicals for Joe Josephson, with Charley writing the book and lyrics. Is married twice. His first wife, Beth Spencer, divorced him in a high-profile case alleging (correctly) adultery with Gussie Josephson. His second wife, Gussie, is about to divorce him on grounds of infidelity with the star of his latest film, Meg.

CHARLES KRINGAS: A playwright. A member of the trio of friends. Graduated from Lake Forest Academy with Franklin and Mary in 1965. Has written the book and lyrics for three musicals for Joe Josephson, with Frank composing the music. He marries Evelyn (whom we never see) sometime between 1957 and 1960.

MARY FLYNN: A writer. A member of the trio of friends. Goes to college in New York. Aspires to be a writer. Has an early book rejected. Eventually becomes a critic. Co-writes 'Frankly Frank' with Charley and Frank. Meets Charley and Frank in 1957 when they take an apartment in the same building where she shares with Evelyn (Charley's future wife). She is hopelessly in love with Frank and tries to reconcile him with Charley after the television incident. Until 1968 does not drink because of an addictive personality. After 1968 is a drunk.

BETH SHEPERD: A singer and performer. Frank's first wife, he marries her after she falls pregnant with his child in 1960. A Texan, long-legged and straight-talking. She has children with Frank. She divorces Frank in 1966 on grounds of infidelity with Gussie Josephson.

You can see from these breakdowns how an agent can take the most important information such as the character's sex/age/voice-type and start to shortlist potential auditionees from their client list. For a completely new production, as in the case of *Mamma Mia!*, the remit might be quite broad as the creative team will probably still be at an early stage in their planning. Ages and even vocal ranges may be changeable according to who walks in the door. For a longer-running show doing a recast, it is likely that the characters' descriptions will be more detailed.

Getting an agent

Agents routinely attend the showcases run by most musical theatre and acting courses.

Find out afterwards who has come to the showcase and if you are one of the performers not approached by an agent, don't despair – it isn't the end of a career that hasn't begun! You could write a brief letter, with CV and photo, saying what part of the showcase you were in. Find out a little bit about each agent, including who they represent. This shows a mature and business-like approach. If you don't hear back after a week or so you could phone. Don't pester – agents are very busy people. If you ask an artist's opinion of their agent, be aware that if that person has been in constant work they will be pleased with the agent. If they have not had many auditions or have not got work, they may "rubbish" the agent. This is difficult to assess – ask a few performers with the same agent and you will get a range of opinions.

Getting an agent without doing a training course is normally more difficult to achieve. If you are in a show, agents will sometimes come to see it and you can approach them afterwards. Or other people in the show may have agents coming, but don't expect them to be helpful and tell you – this is a competitive business!

How to get an audition

This can be the most frustrating part of the musical-theatre industry. In the majority of cases, your agent will be the person who gets you an audition. Aside from negotiating your contract, this is one of the main reasons to have an agent. It can be hard not being sent up for a role that many of your colleagues are being seen for. However, if the agent sends unsuitable people they will lose the trust of the person handling the casting.

If you feel very strongly that you are right for a role, there is no harm in calling up your agent to discuss it with them. Agents work hard for you but don't expect them to do all the work; a good working relationship is important. Let them know what work you would like to do. But don't phone them every day – it can create the impression that you don't trust them. Also remember that if they are on the phone to their clients all the time, they can't get on with their job. Telephone them when you hear of a role which might be right for you or a planned production that you know about, and ask how you can help get an audition. Bear in mind they will probably already know about the production through their own sources.

Always keep your eye on the classified ads in *The Stage* and other publications (see page 133) as these may list jobs unknown to your agent.

A note on open auditions

From time to time open auditions may be advertised, usually in *The Stage* or a local paper. Most often these are in London, but may also sometimes be in Manchester, Cardiff, Birmingham or any other major city.

Open auditions sometimes turn up unexpected talents – for example, Laura Michelle Kelly, who won an Olivier for her portrayal of Mary Poppins, began her career by trying out for *Beauty and the Beast* at an open audition. Dave Willetts, who had enormous success as both Jean Valjean and the Phantom, was discovered at an open audition. Their talent was recognised and that started them on very successful careers.

On the day of an open audition, you should arrive really early. Usually, you will be given a number and asked to wait in a queue; this is where the mind games can start – don't be put off by people around you talking up what they have or haven't done. Having waited to be seen, sometimes for a long time, the mental energy to walk on stage and immediately show something of yourself isn't easy, but it is possible. Be aware that you might be asked to sing only sixteen bars. This is when it really does feel like a meat market.

In an open audition it is crucially important to have a song which shows something about you immediately. Good examples of this are "There's gotta be something better than this" from *Sweet Charity* or "Anthem" from *Chess*, both of which show much about your personality and voice by the end of the first page.

A tip from a student:

> *I have bought a three-legged lightweight stool that I now carry to open auditions. Standing for eight hours or more is exhausting when you're expected to give your best if and when you eventually go in. Also, take a thermos – hot chocolate in winter and a cool drink in summer. It helps to keep your spirits up.*

Reality TV programmes

Whatever your own thoughts are on reality TV casting, these will probably be around for some time – celebrity is very much in vogue. Should you audition for them? This is entirely a personal decision.

Advantages:

- If it works well for you then it leads to instant fame and exposure to the industry.

- It can provide an opportunity to work with top professionals.

- Even if you don't win, contestants who get through to the final few programmes are often offered roles on other shows.

Disadvantages:

- There is always a possibility of harming your career if you are not shown well. You have no control over editing (how the programme shots are put together).

- You don't necessarily have a choice in selecting what song you sing.

- In the later stages of the process you will probably work under pressure to the point of emotional and physical exhaustion, which will be filmed.

This sounds harsh, but it has been the experience of some of my students, so be aware of these points and decide whether it's for you. I've also had some performers for whom it has been the launch of a career and an enjoyable experience. It's a hard decision.

TV shows and public expectations have made it all the more difficult for performers. It is a fact of life that audiences often come to see a favourite performer. The reality of this, like it or not, is that shows will, most of the time, run longer as a result.

David Grindrod (casting director)

Photos and CVs

Once you are put forward for a role, the first point of contact with the casting director and creative team will be your headshot and CV. It is vital that these represent you well and accurately.

Photos

A photograph should be as natural as possible and truly represent you.

- Wear clothes you are comfortable in and take a change of clothes to the photo shoot so that you can try different images.
- Avoid cluttering your neckline – it is distracting.
- Be aware that backgrounds create a different image of you, and can be distracting.

Don't "touch up" a photograph. Artists arriving at auditions are often unrecognisable from their photo – which is not a good idea.

After a photographic session, you will usually be given a computer disc or contact sheet with many photos to choose from. It is better to have some other opinions before you make the final choice. If you have an agent, they will usually have a strong idea about which photo should represent you.

Make sure that your chosen headshots are contrasting – for example, hair up/hair down for girls, casual/formal for boys. A hairstyle with a heavy fringe, or falling over your face, should be avoided – your eyes are very important and should convey a lot about you.

CVs

Name: you should make your name stand out in **bold type**.

Address and telephone number: again, **bold type**. Add voicemail, email and mobile number. Make sure you can be contacted easily day and night, and check your messages regularly!

Training: if you have been to a recognised training course, include it on your CV. Also include any ongoing training, either in private lessons or at places such as the Actors' Centre – it shows a good attitude and awareness of professional development.

> *I always expect performers to be continuously developing themselves.*
>
> Trevor Jackson (casting director)

Experience: don't be tempted to exaggerate your professional experience too much – we've all been tempted to upgrade the end-of-year show into the Palladium on our CVs, but be aware that the theatre world is very small and you may be asked to substantiate your claims.

Many people at the start of their professional careers ask me if they should include non-professional roles on their CV. In general, if you have had professional training it is not necessary to include amateur productions you may have been involved in before then. But do include all roles played while training, as well as the names of the directors, choreographers and MDs you worked with.

A performer's CV should only be one side of A4. You should include a brief profile to explain what musical styles you can sing: for example, jazz, rock/pop, opera, etc. Your CV should include:

- Scanned photo
- Your name and contact information
- Agent's name
- Spotlight and Equity numbers
- Personal details – height, playing age, build, hair colour
- Training
- Voice type (soprano, mezzo, tenor, baritone or bass) and range
- Theatre experience
- Television experience
- Film experience
- Skills
- Accents

Although it can be difficult to describe your singing voice in a CV – particularly if you can sing in many styles – it is important for a casting agent to have some information. If you decide to include a CD, make sure it is a good recording of no more than three songs, each of around a minute.

Depending on your experience, your CV might look something like this:

Notes on writing letters

In this email age you would be surprised at the power of a polite, well-written letter. Here are some thoughts:

1) Aim to write a letter that attracts an agent's or a director's interest.

2) Write the person's full name (e.g. Dear Sir Cameron Mackintosh) – not Mr/Ms or first name only.

3) Make sure your letter is brief and to the point (and don't whinge!).

4) Enthusiasm and positivity are always valued.

5) When to write? – when you see a job advertised or hear about it through other performers; when you feel you are genuinely right for a job (try to be objective).

Demo recordings, videos and showreels

These allow an agent or casting director to hear short examples of different singing styles. Keep your examples short and try to choose songs that have an impact within 32 bars – so keep piano introductions short. Your choices should be as contrasting as possible, but make sure they really do suit you – work to your strengths and put your best track first, otherwise they won't bother to listen to the rest. Always include a CV and photo.

A good example of a female demo might be:

- "I could have danced all night" from *My Fair Lady*. By the second phrase they'll know if you have a "legit" (see page 35) soprano voice or not and whether they need to listen to any more.

- "Arthur in the afternoon" from *The Act*. Funny – a good song to show your acting ability and more of a speech quality to your voice.

- A pop song of your choice. You could use a backing track for this. Make sure it shows some range.

For a male:

- "Younger than springtime" from *South Pacific* – but only if you really can sing it! The first page will be enough for the panel to judge if you're good at this style.
- "The Masochism Tango" by Tom Lehrer. This makes good use of language and can show a quirky side of your character.
- A pop song of your choice. You could use a backing track for this. Make sure it shows some range.

N.B. If you use backing tracks for all of your songs – which is possible these days – your interpretation will be influenced by someone else's idea of tempo and phrasing. If you can organise and afford it, use a pianist for most of the songs.

Heartfelt comment from an agent:

Make sure you always include the right postage on the envelope. I don't take kindly to having to go to the post office to collect a package on which I need to pay a £2 surcharge. You wouldn't fancy your chances after that!

It is getting more and more normal for artists to have a video or DVD showreel. This should contain short excerpts of any professional work you have done. Videos made by you or your colleagues aren't usually of good enough quality to get you work. It is worth spending money – try to see examples of other people's videos to see what you think looks good.

Comment from an agent:

From a personal point of view, I prefer a CD from singers rather than a DVD. If I like the voice then I'll bring them in for an interview.

What to wear

There are endless theories/ideas about what to wear. Mine are the result of observation! Most importantly, you should feel comfortable in what you are wearing. I think many people would own up to having something "lucky" that they wear – theatre is full of superstition. If you feel that wearing something particular helps you, then wear it.

I think, above all, you should dress with respect for the occasion and try to judge whether casual or more formal dress is appropriate. Often, actors who I work with will come into their lesson dressed in their audition gear so that they have another pair of eyes to check it over. I've had years of seeing what works and what doesn't. Here are a few ideas.

Dressing for the part

Is it necessary to dress specifically for the part for which I'm auditioning? Directors and casting directors don't always have time to imagine you in the part. You can help them by approximating to the style of the show, so a bit of research on the internet might be useful. For example, if you are auditioning for the role of Mary Poppins, it may not be appropriate to wear stilettos and a mini-skirt! Similarly, for Tony in *West Side Story* a suit and tie doesn't suggest his social background. Your talent may transcend this; however, it might help if you wear a frock for Mary Poppins and maybe a leather jacket for Tony. This may seem like stereotyping, but it can sometimes give the director's imagination a helping hand on a long day of auditions.

When *Les Misérables* first auditioned many years ago, everyone who went for the role of Eponine turned up in a cloth cap and a long coat. I really don't think that's necessary anymore, but again you can help the director by wearing maybe a mid-calf skirt or a simple dress which suggests the period of the show.

Trevor Jackson (Cameron Mackintosh's casting director) suggests a jacket for boys for *The Phantom of the Opera* – "a full suit can make you look a bit like an insurance salesman." And, for *Miss Saigon*, "quasi-military clothing can give the idea that you could be suitable."

If you aren't sure what character you're auditioning for, or if it's a new show, I personally like someone who dresses with a flair for expressing something about their personality. Through trial and error, you can find something that makes you memorable – and it doesn't have to cost a lot. If you search stalls for unusual T-shirts, shirts, dresses or jewellery, you can often find a bargain.

In London, it is quite possible to find relatively inexpensive hand-made clothes that will make you more memorable than if you turn up in the latest high-street brand. Charity shops are worth a rummage.

If you are recalled for an audition, it can be a good idea to wear the same clothes to help refresh the casting director's memory. This isn't so necessary if you are already known to them.

Look at your body-type and wear something that shows you well on stage. Current fashion for girls at the time of writing is to wear figure-hugging tops exposing a lot of bare flesh. This can look good in 'life' but not always on stage – be critical and look at yourself from the back as well as the front. Make sure jewellery is not distracting – and no logos on T-shirts. We want them to notice *you*.

Hipster trousers, both for men and women, don't always flatter your leg-length on stage. Waist-high trousers and jeans give you a longer leg and make them look great! Men: it's not a good idea to wear shorts – auditioning is a more formal occasion than that!

Here are a few suggestions which could form the basis of your wardrobe:

Boys could have in their wardrobe:

- A pair of well-cut jeans
- Dark trousers
- A smart jacket that goes with everything
- A tie! (just in case)
- T-shirts in colours that suit your skin tone – especially under unflattering working lights on stage or fluorescent lights in a studio
- Smart shoes/trainers
- Plain shirts in different colours, including white

I suggest something memorable like an electric blue or vivid red T-shirt/shirt – you will know what suits you. If you have a fair complexion, be aware that colours like pale yellow or orange can drain the colour from your face.

Girls could have:

- Skirts of three different lengths: mini (if you really do have the legs!); knee-length; calf-length
- Smart trousers
- Well-cut jeans
- Jacket

- A white and a black top
- T-shirts in colours that suit your skin tone – especially under unflattering working lights on stage or fluorescent lights in a studio
- Jewellery to express individuality

Shoes

Shoes are REALLY important. Ladies in particular should practise singing and moving in their audition shoes – especially if they have high heels. Heels throw you off balance and, if you're not careful, your neck extends and your head (a third of your bodyweight) thrusts forward to balance you. Imagine the constriction this puts on your neck and subsequently your larynx. Your voice could sound thinner than usual – it really can make that amount of difference. So **practise in your shoes!**

Men seem mostly to wear informal shoes or trainers – I personally quite like the mixture of smart clothes and trainers – the combination is quite sexy! However, make sure that your shoes aren't too loose and floppy. If you haven't tried socks with your shoes, try them on the night before, otherwise you might find yourself crossing the stage with tight shoes that pinch – not the best thing for focus (this was one of my student's experiences).

Hair

Ideally *clean!*

As mentioned on page 18, be careful that hair doesn't obscure your face and cover your eyes. Matt Ryan, a director with whom I've worked on many projects, always says, "The eyes are the mirror to the soul."

If your hair is your crowning glory, then a possibility might be to go into your audition with it tied back then casually untie it and shake it out at an opportune moment!

This information may appear over-prescriptive but, like everything, it only becomes obvious once you've done it wrong. It's best to find these things out before you make a wrong decision which throws you – however slightly – on your important day.

Choosing a song

In the audition brief, you will be given information about the kind of material you will need. You should select at least two songs that you feel are suitable. However, in addition to these, you should always take a selection of other material with you in your folder. Make sure you are equally comfortable with all of them or the panel may choose the one you are least sure of – I have been in so many auditions where the auditionee hasn't done themselves justice simply because the MD or director chose a song that wasn't sufficiently prepared. You may think you know a song well, but unless you've worked on it recently you may get a nasty shock when it comes to performing it.

Ideally you should have, at any one time, a minimum of six songs you know inside out; all of them in different styles and from different composers.

Trevor Jackson (casting director)

As an actor, you should be prepared to audition with a minimum amount of notice. Your agent might call you the night before with an audition if a casting director finds some space in the schedule. Even if you don't have time to prepare a song specifically for the occasion, you should be able to find something useful in your folder that will at least show an appropriate voice quality and something about you as an actor.

The most essential consideration when choosing what material to take to an audition is the musical style – both genre and era – of the project. Above all else, identifying the musical style will affect your selection of song, vocal colour and acting choices. Very often, the casting director will specify the style of the piece when sending out the audition information and you should consider this carefully and do your research. While this may seem obvious, you would be surprised how many people come in with a pop song for a *Showboat* audition, to quote an extreme example. Casting directors want performers who make intelligent and informed choices.

Is it a good idea to do songs from the show you are auditioning for? There is no hard-and-fast rule for this. The danger of singing material from the show is that you may do it very differently from the way the director and MD have conceived it. On the other hand, I've often heard directors say that they wish somebody *would* sing one of the songs, so it depends on the creative team. Try to offer a choice and let the panel decide.

Is it a good idea to perform your own songs? Don't use your own material. Also, songs from new shows are generally not the best choice to show you off. The panel will probably judge the material rather than you.

Material for a recall audition (a call-back)

A recall audition after an open audition This really counts as a first audition. You should take back the song you sang at the open audition and a choice of two other contrasting songs.

A recall audition after your first private audition Often, you will be asked to bring the same song or a suggestion will be offered at your first audition of something else the panel need to hear. You should certainly bring your portfolio of music and give them a wide choice.

New musicals If you have been given music to learn, you should memorise it. Sometimes you will be given a CD with the accompaniment of the song; more often than not, you will only have the sheet music – possibly only one or two days before your audition – and you will be expected to find a way to learn it. The excuse "I couldn't find anyone to play it through" may be true but I'm afraid isn't acceptable. For this reason, you should always keep the names and telephone numbers of a number of coaches handy.

Some musicals recall up to six times. After the initial pleasure of being recalled, it is increasingly hard to keep focused as the stakes get higher. Really listen to what is being asked of you. It can be quite draining to go through this experience but it is also fantastic to know that you are being considered so seriously. At this stage, it is still a lottery. Casting can be quite a lengthy process and you can't really "game-plan" what the director is thinking. It depends on the dynamic of the final mix of auditionees and this can change at the last moment. You can tie yourself in knots interpreting a look – just stay clear-headed. Somewhere there is a part with your name on it, waiting for you.

Song classifications

In many cases a casting director will request from agents that their clients bring two songs – an up-tempo song and a ballad. Occasionally, they may be more specific and dictate more precisely the kind of material they would like to hear. Here is a guide to the styles they may request.

Narrative

A narrative song tells a story. Narrative songs can be in the third-person, such as Kander and Ebb's "Ring them bells", or the first-person, as in Jason Robert Brown's "Stars and the moon". The synopsis might span a single day, as in "A trip to the library" from *She Loves Me*, or a whole lifetime, as in "Liaisons" from *A Little Night Music*. The listener should be taken on a dramatic journey and your voice should be coloured by specific changing thoughts. For this reason, narrative songs are really useful in an audition as they allow you to show a wide range of different emotions and vocal colours. As a starting point, you could listen to Maltby and Shires' *Closer than ever*, Stephen Schwartz's *Godspell* and *Children of Eden*, or Jason Robert Brown's *Songs for a New World*. Pop songs can also have strong narratives – think of Elton John's *Daniel*, Bruce Springsteen's *The River* or Alanis Morissette's *Ironic*.

Comedy

A song with witty language will often require speech quality, although that's not necessarily the case. Songs such as "Glitter and be gay" from *Candide*, or "Love I hear" from *A Funny Thing Happened on the Way to the Forum*, for example, allow you to show off both your voice and your funny side. When choosing a comedy song, think of what makes you laugh. If you find the material amusing, you stand much more chance of cheering up a weary panel of creatives. If you are planning to use a specific accent for your song, first practise in your own accent to find the comedic sense. Victoria Wood, *Fascinating Aïda* and Tom Lehrer volumes are all great sources of material. The era of Cole Porter, Irving Berlin and Noël Coward are also packed with clever and witty lyrics and are surprisingly under-used in auditions. For more contemporary material, look at Lopez and Marx's *Avenue Q*. Another good source is the Goldrich and Heisler songbook, which includes modern numbers for women – a real find.

N.B. It is risky and not necessarily useful to do really fast patter songs in an audition. Apart from showing your linguistic virtuosity, they rarely allow for any other qualities to shine through and they can also be tricky to co-ordinate with the pianist.

Also see the **Music hall** section on page 37.

Ballad

A ballad usually has more vocal line and would generally be an opportunity to show your singing voice – though of course not at the expense of the language. There are a vast number of ballads to choose from – love songs, songs about loss – the list is absolutely endless. Above all, when working on your ballad, avoid being self-indulgent – over-sentimentality isn't attractive to a panel. A ballad can very easily be one-dimensional and subsequently show a limited spectrum of vocal colour: this isn't an effective use of your time in the audition. Are there any long repeated sections of music in your ballad – do they need to be there and are they vital to the story? Be strict with yourself. Some good examples of ballads with a range of emotional colour might include Andrew Lippa's "I'll be here", Kander and Ebb's "A quiet thing" and Rodgers and Hammerstein's "This nearly was mine". Lesser-known contemporary American composers such as Craig Carnelia and John Bucchino are also worth a look. There are a number of what I would call "power-ballads" which are useful if you are auditioning for a role with high-octane vocal demands – think of Boublil and Schönberg's "Why God, why?" from *Miss Saigon*, "As long as he needs me" from *Oliver*, or "Daddy's son" from *Ragtime*.

Jazz

Surprisingly, jazz songs can be the hardest to pull off in an audition situation. No microphone, a piano accompaniment which may not be what you are expecting, and the apparent formality of the audition situation can all work against you. Try and find a jazz song with some sense of narrative or character which will appeal to you as an actor. For example:

Choosing a song

"Cry me a river", "God bless the child", "Ain't misbehavin'" or "The Girl from Ipanema". Once you have chosen your song, make sure you have a well-written-out piano accompaniment. Do not rely on a lead sheet which has just the vocal line and chords, as the pianist may not be comfortable with improvising from chord symbols. Remember – the more information you give your pianist to work from the more you can expect to recognise what they play. As with all songs, be careful not to copy well-known singers but make sure that you express *your* personality. A really good place to start is the great American songbook – many standards actually started life as theatre songs. Look at Rodgers and Hart's "There's a small hotel", the Gershwins' "Nice work if you can get it" or Arlen's "A sleepin' bee".

Torch song

This is quite a specific genre but one that seems to crop up from time to time on casting breakdowns. Almost certainly songs of loss, torch songs are usually associated with the great female artists such as Edith Piaf or Judy Garland and are also sometimes referred to as "the eleven o'clock number". Examples include Arlen's "The man that got away" and Kander and Ebb's "Maybe this time". There is great skill required in putting across these numbers without a sense of self-pity and you will help yourself greatly by building intensity gradually and not peaking too soon – leave yourself somewhere to go emotionally and vocally.

Up-tempo

Up-tempo denotes any song with drive and rhythmic energy, without necessarily being wordy. When working on your song, ask yourself why the composer has chosen to adopt a fast tempo. Is it youthful exuberance, as in "Don't rain on my parade" from *Funny Girl*, bubbling expectation as in "Luck be a lady" from *Guys and Dolls*, or sheer anger as in "I don't remember Christmas" from *Closer than Ever?* Your up-tempo song will probably be one of the hardest to choose – once you have found one that suits you and shows you well, look after it.

"Legit"

This word (short for "legitimate") is very widely used by casting directors and denotes what we might think of as more classical (or "light classical") voice production. Particularly called upon for period pieces such as Rodgers and Hammerstein shows, a panel will be listening for your ability to work with language within a smooth vocal line. Increasingly, opera companies are broadening their repertoire and programming musical-theatre pieces and will want to hear "legit" repertoire. As a starting point, try Rodgers and Hart, Rodgers and Hammerstein, Kurt Weill, Gershwin (particularly *Porgy and Bess*) and Marc Blitzstein shows.

N.B. If you are working from an anthology or "best of" album, check if the key has been altered from the original score. The panel may ask you to sing it in the original key, which may feel very different – to sound your very best, a song needs to be muscularly worked into your voice in a particular key.

Operatic

Similar to "legit", there are many roles in musical theatre that normally demand a more operatic technique. Examples can be found in *She Loves Me, Jerry Springer: The Opera, Candide* and *The Phantom of the Opera*, to name but a few. Once again, it is your task as a musical-theatre performer to show off the required "money notes" (the colloquial term for high, full-sounding notes which excite the audience) and vocal line while still giving full service to the lyrics. It is useful to have an operatic aria in English in your folder, if you can sing it.

Rock/pop

The past 30 years have seen the emergence of rock music as an exciting and powerful theatrical language. Shows such as *Jesus Christ Superstar*, *Hair* and *Rent* have changed the musical landscape and brought with them new vocal and acting demands. At the time of writing, the West End is awash with compilation shows based on the back catalogue of pop bands and recording artists. As well as exploring songs in the rock musical repertoire, you could look at songs by Queen or Elton John, which usually have an innate theatricality about them. Think of Elton John's "Your song", Barbra Streisand's "Evergreen" or Queen's "I'm going slightly mad", all of which have finely crafted and interesting lyrics that allow you to show your acting side as well as a rock/pop vocal sound. But, as with jazz songs, it can be hard to create the effect you are after with just piano accompaniment and no microphone.

Specific composers (e.g. "Bring a Sondheim")

For composers such as Sondheim or Kurt Weill, who have very distinctive and individual writing styles, a creative team might specifically ask for examples of their repertoire. Obviously, you won't be able to cover all bases on this front and you may need to do a quick-learn (though this is never ideal) if you are asked for a piece by a composer not in your folder. Generally, however, I would suggest it useful for you to have a Sondheim and a Rodgers and Hammerstein song at hand as these tend to be the most requested. In any case, they are great learning tools.

Character song

This is a very broad remit which I would suggest describes any song that demands some kind of heightened or exaggerated characterisation. This may be anything from a comic accent as in "Easily assimilated" from *Candide*, neuroticism in "Tonight at eight" from *She Loves Me*, or overblown romanticism as in "Suddenly Seymour" from *Little Shop of Horrors*. Cockney and music-hall (see below) are a rich source of character songs.

Cockney

As well as the many musicals written in cockney dialect, such as *Oliver* and *Half a Sixpence*, it is quite common for actors auditioning for straight plays with some music in them to be asked to sing a short burst of a cockney song in their audition. *Mother Clap's Molly House* and *The Threepenny Opera*, both recently produced at the National Theatre, called for actors who could sing in a cockney dialect. Don't just go for the most obvious choices – "My old man" and "Why am I always the bridesmaid?" – there are literally thousands of brilliant cockney songs for you to choose from.

Music hall

Often, though not always, in a cockney dialect, music-hall songs are usually witty character songs, useful for showing off your use of language. The fact that they are so rarely performed these days is definitely in your favour at an audition – nothing will please a panel more after a long day than a short, well-delivered comic song that they've never heard before. If you've never heard recordings of artists such as George Formby and Stanley Holloway, look them up at the library or online as they are well worth a listen.

Contemporary

This is obviously an ever-shifting category and it is important for you to keep up-to-date with new material/composers. If you've been in the profession a while, ask yourself when was the last time you learned a new audition song. Is it time to try something new? At the time of writing, composers such as Jason Robert Brown, Stiles and Drewe, Michael John LaChiusa, Adam Guettel, Georgia Stitt and Scott Alan have all emerged in the last ten years and would be considered "contemporary". If you find it hard to know where to start in terms of new repertoire, why not go along to some cabarets where many such songs are showcased, or find yourself a coach who has their finger on the pulse.

Repertoire

Here are suggestions of volumes that would make a good start to your music collection. Some of them may well be available in your local public library. Otherwise they could become part of your Christmas/birthday present list:

100 Years of Popular Music. Imperial Publishing.
20 volumes: 2 volumes for each decade 1900–2000
Alfred's Singers Library of Musical Theatre. Alfred Publishing.
Volumes 1–2 (soprano; mezzo/alto; tenor; baritone/bass)
These volumes give synopses of shows and – very usefully – suggestions for 16-bar excerpts for audition purposes
Audition Songs for Professional Singers. Wise Publications (Music Sales).
Boys; girls; pop hits
Contemporary Singing Actor. Hal Leonard.
4 volumes (2 men, 2 women)
Singer's Musical Theatre Anthology. Hal Leonard Publishing.
Volumes 1–5 (soprano; mezzo-soprano/belter; tenor; baritone/bass
Songs in their original keys from musicals
Accompaniment CDs available

The Actor's Songbook. Hal Leonard Publishing.
    2 volumes (men; women): character/comedy songs
The "Best of" series. Imperial Publishing.
    Cole Porter; Irving Berlin; George Gershwin
The Music Vault. Warner Bros.
    Sheet music from the archives (copies normally out of
    circulation)
Ahrens and Flaherty Songbook. Warner Bros (Imperial).
All Sondheim. Warner Bros.
    4 volumes
Andrew Lloyd Webber Anthology. Really Useful Group.
Brecht/Eisler Songbook. Oak Publications (Music Sales).
Hey Look Me Over – Cy Coleman's Broadway Showstoppers. Imperial
    Publishing.
Jerome Kern Collection. Hal Leonard.
Kander and Ebb Collection. Hal Leonard.
Kurt Weill Songs – a Centennial Anthology. Alfred Publications
    (Imperial).
    2 volumes
Leonard Bernstein Song Album. Boosey and Hawkes.
Marc Blitzstein Songbook. Boosey and Hawkes.
Rodgers and Hammerstein Collection. Williamson Music (Hal
    Leonard).
Rodgers and Hart American Muscial Theatre Anthology. Hal
    Leonard.
The Comden and Green Songbook. Warner Bros.
The Jason Robert Brown Collection. Hal Leonard.
The Legendary Musicals of Boublil and Schönberg. Wise Publications
    (Music Sales).
The Stephen Schwartz Songbook. Imperial Publishing.

N.B. Many songbooks now have accompanying CDs – useful
in many ways, but at an audition you will normally sing to
live piano accompaniment which can be a shock if you haven't
had the opportunity to go through it with a live pianist.

A useful starting point . . .

I asked some of the people who study with me for a few of their most useful audition songs: those they have found serve them well. This is just to start you thinking:

Guys

"A piece of the action" from *The Life* (Coleman)
"A quiet girl" from *Wonderful Town* (Bernstein)
"Anthem" from *Chess* (Ulvaeus and Andersson)
"Being alive" from *Company* (Sondheim)
"Charles Atlas Song (I can make you a man)" from *The Rocky Horror Show* (O'Brien)
"Come fly with me" (van Heusen)
"Comfort and joy" from *Bat Boy: The Musical* (O'Keefe)
"Copacabana" from *Copacabana* (Manilow, Feldman and Sussman)
"Dancing through life" from *Wicked* (Schwartz)
"Don't take much" from *The Life* (Coleman)
"Go the distance" from *Hercules* (Menken)
"Guido's Song" from *Nine* (Yeston)
"Have I told you lately" (Morrison)
"Heaven" from *A Night in Heaven* (Adams and Vallance)
"Heaven on their minds" from *Jesus Christ Superstar* (Lloyd Webber)
"High flying adored" from *Evita* (Lloyd Webber)
"I am what I am" from *La Cage aux Folles* (Herman)
"I can't stand still" from *Footloose* (Snow)
"I don't believe in heroes anymore" from *Three Guys Naked from the Waist Down* (Rupert)
"I don't remember you" from *The Happy Time* (Kander)
"I want to break free" from *We Will Rock You* (Deacon)
"I will make you proud" from *Martin Guerre* (Schönberg)
"If I didn't believe in you" from *The Last Five Years* (Brown)

"If I loved you" from *Carousel* (Rodgers)
"If I sing" from *Closer Than Ever* (Shire)
"If you can find me I'm here" from *Evening Primrose* (Sondheim)
"In my place" (Berryman, Buckland, Champion and Martin)
   Coldplay
"It don't mean a thing (if it ain't got that swing)" (Ellington)
"It's hard to speak my heart" from *Parade* (Brown)
"La chanson de Jacky" (Brel)
"Larger than life" from *My Favorite Year* (Flaherty)
"Last one picked" from *Whoop-Dee-Doo!* (Gallagher)
"Mama, a rainbow" from *Minnie's Boys* (Grossmann)
"New words" from *In the Beginning* (Yeston)
"On Broadway" from *Smokey Joe's Cafe* (Leiber and Stoller)
"Proud lady" from *The Baker's Wife* (Schwartz)
"Real big news" from *Parade* (Brown)
"Satin doll" (Ellington, Mercer and Strayhorn)
"Sensitive Song" from *Cops: The Musical* (O'Keefe)
"She loves me" from *She Loves Me* (Bock)
"She's always a woman" (Joel)
"Shiksa Goddess" from *The Last Five Years* (Brown)
"Springtime for Hitler" from *The Producers* (Brooks and Kelly)
"Suspicious minds" (Zambon)
"The kid inside" from *Is there Life after High School?* (Carnelia)
"The Masochism Tango" (Lehrer)
"The river won't flow" from *Songs for a New World* (Brown)
"This joint is jumpin'" (Waller)
"Tonight at eight" from *She Loves Me* (Bock)
"Use what you got" from *The Life* (Coleman)
"What you'd call a dream" from *Diamonds* (Carnelia)
"What you own" from *Rent* (Larson)
"Wick" from *The Secret Garden* (Simon)
"Winter's on the wing" from *The Secret Garden* (Simon)
"Woman" (Lennon)

Girls

"A summer in Ohio" from *The Last Five Years* (Brown)
"All for you" from *Seussical the Musical* (Flaherty)
"Crazy for you" from *Vision Quest* (Lind)
"Dancing with the fools" from *Rags* (Strouse)
"Disneyland" from *Smile* (Hamlisch)
"Fascinating rhythm" from *Lady, Be Good* (Gershwin)
"Flashdance... What a feeling" from *Flashdance* (Moroder)
"Funny girl" from *Funny Girl* (Styne)
"Good morning Baltimore" from *Hairspray* (Shaiman)
"Holding to the ground" from *Falsettoland* (Finn)
"I could have danced all night" from *My Fair Lady* (Loewe)
"I have confidence" from *The Sound of Music* (Rodgers)
"I will be loved tonight" from *I Love You, You're Perfect, Now Change* (Roberts)
"I wish I could forget you" from *Passion* (Sondheim)
"In my own little corner" from *Cinderella* (Rodgers)
"Just like a pill" (Moore and Austin)
"Maybe I like it this way" from *The Wild Party* (Lippa)
"Mister Snow" from *Carousel* (Rodgers)
"No more tears (enough is enough)" (Jabara and Roberts)
"Patterns" from *Closer than Ever* (Shire)
"Piano practicing" (Welch and Welch)
"Popular" from *Wicked* (Schwartz)
"Raunchy" from *110 in the Shade* (Schmidt)
"Science fiction" from *The Rocky Horror Show* (O'Brien)
"Shadowland" from *The Lion King* (Zimmer, Morake and Mancina)
"Someone else's story" from *Chess* (Ulvaeus and Andersson)
"Someone like you" from *Jekyll & Hyde* (Wildhorn)
"Someone to watch over me" from *Crazy for You* (Gershwin)
"Still hurting" from *The Last Five Years* (Brown)
"Surabaya Johnny" from *Happy End* (Weill)

"Taylor, the latte boy" (Goldrich)
"Tell me on a Sunday" from *Song and Dance* (Lloyd Webber)
"The miller's son" from *A Little Night Music* (Sondheim)
"The music that makes me dance" from *Funny Girl* (Styne)
"The nearness of you" (Carmichael)
"The spark of creation" from *Children of Eden* (Schwartz)
"There's a fine, fine line" from *Avenue Q* (Lopez and Marx)
"This place is mine" from *Phantom* (Yeston)
"Tom" from *Hello Again* (LaChiusa)
"Unusual way" from *Nine* (Yeston)
"What I did for love" from *A Chorus Line* (Hamlisch)
"What kind of fool" from *Saturday Night Fever* (Galuten and Gibb)
"What's the use of wond'rin'?" from *Carousel* (Rodgers)
"You don't know this man" from *Parade* (Brown)

This is a random and eclectic mix of songs suggested by young performers. I've included it to show how many musicals are out there to be explored.

Listening to and watching CDs and DVDs

This is obviously a good way to familiarise yourself with repertoire and learn from great performers. The danger is that you may copy the performances rather than form your own interpretation. If possible, start by playing your song from the score yourself – or get someone to play it for you. Then maybe refer to a recording for stylistic ideas. Remember – there is no substitute for undertaking the detailed analytical work yourself.

The internet affords lots of opportunities to watch and download (make sure it's legal) performances. Sites such as

YouTube often have multiple performances of the same song by different performers.

Preparing your sheet music

Cuts

The audition panel will be working to a tight schedule and often doesn't have time to hear verses that simply repeat and/ or don't develop musically. You could prepare two versions of the same song – one shorter version for round one and the full version for a recall. For a first audition, your performance should ideally last no more than two minutes. This can, of course, vary slightly either way, but you may need to cut some of the song. This is a bigger subject than simply putting a pencil mark through the page:

- Does the story make sense if you cut some of it?

- Does the harmony make sense if you go from one point of the song to another? If the cut straddles a key-change, you may need to think again.

- If there are repeats, do you need to do them? It can be a good idea to go straight to the second-time bar if the story does not get lost.

As an example of how you might cut part of a song, let's look at "Easy as life" from Disney's *Aida*. This is a good song for a first audition, with a strong rhythmic drive that really allows you to make an impact straight away.

Aida has a wonderful opening statement:

> *This is the moment when the gods expect me to beg for help*
> *But I won't even try*
> *I want nothing in the world but*

Myself, to protect me
And I won't lie down
Roll over and die.
All I have to do is forget how much I love him;
All I have to do is put my longing to one side
Tell myself that love's an ever-changing situation
Passion would have cooled
And all the magic would have died
It's easy, it's easy as life

The punchy and interesting opening statement should make the panel want to listen to you. The music then repeats, but the lyric doesn't really tell us anything new and the emotional colour doesn't change, giving little scope for showing different vocal qualities. So, for the purposes of a first audition, you could sing the opening verse and then cut from "It's easy, it's easy as life" in the first verse to where it is repeated in the second, and from there continue to the end (i.e. bar 72 becomes bar 119). This allows you to move on dramatically and vocally.

It is part of your job to assess which parts of the text are vital to make sense of the linear narrative and which might be surplus to requirement in an audition situation. Above all, try out your cuts with a pianist beforehand and make sure they work. Don't let there be a nasty surprise at the audition!

Sixteen bars of your best   This is the phrase that strikes fear in the heart of all actors. Unfortunately, creative teams often run short of time and asking for "sixteen bars of your best" allows them to get an idea if they are interested in somebody. As I mentioned in the section on open auditions, it is a skill in itself to be able to show what you can do in such a short space of time. Choose a short section of one of your songs that allows you to reach a vocal and emotional climax (which is often towards the end of a song).

I suggest you always have at least two extracts like this in your folder. If you haven't sorted it out in advance, the best person to ask is the pianist – but it's much better to have prepared it in advance.

How to help the pianist

There have already been some references in this book to the subject of the pianist. How can you help them do the best job for you? This is a reversal of the train of thought I often hear: "They played too loud/missed the repeat…" It is up to you to explain what it is you need. Bear in mind that the pianist sits in the audition room for hours at a time and has to cope with all sorts of accompaniments. You could consider taking your own accompanist if your song is particularly difficult or if doing so makes you feel more confident. But if you do use the official pianist, be realistic about what you can expect – however good they are, some pieces are difficult to accompany without having a run-through first.

I've always called the piano accompaniment an "umbilical chord" – cut it and you feel cut adrift. With this in mind it is a good idea to:

1) Practise standing at different distances from the piano. Learn to listen to the accompaniment from different places.

2) Make sure you've heard the actual accompaniment exactly as written and not with the tune doubled. It will come as an unwelcome shock if you hear a separate accompaniment for the first time in the audition.

3) Make sure the music is in the right key for you – NEVER EXPECT THE PIANIST TO TRANSPOSE AT SIGHT. Even if they can

do this, they won't be able to listen to you as effectively and it will be harder for them to accompany you. Pay an arranger to do it in advance, if necessary – a good return for a little investment, and one which will last a lifetime. There are also websites where you can download songs in any key. Make sure you practise your song in the key in which your music is printed as even a semitone can feel very different to sing.

4) Make sure you have a clear copy of your music – not scribbled over with coaching marks or chord symbols.

5) Normally, two bars of introduction (four at the most) are enough before you start singing. If there is a long rest in the voice line, make sure you cut it down, otherwise the panel might stop you. Some books include suggestions for cuts (see page 38).

6) Mark very clearly the following – preferably in a coloured pen or pencil so they really stand out:

- Starting tempo
- Any changes of tempo (including rall, accel, etc.)
- Dynamics and accents
- Any *colla voce* ("follow the voice") sections – these can also be marked "rubato"
- Coda and repeats

7) Present your music so it doesn't fall off the piano and has no difficult page-turns. You can

use a folder with non-reflective plastic sheets that are easy to turn, or stick each page together and then concertina them.

8) Give the right tempo of a song: a useful tip for remembering tempo is to have the accompaniment of the song on an ipod or something similar and play it while you are waiting. Also, walk around – or down the road – at the speed of the song. You must be able to give the pianist an accurate tempo, in spite of being nervous and/or excited. I have found that the major complaint of auditionees is: "He/she played it too fast/too slow." It is your responsibility to give the right tempo.

Sometimes a pianist can get it wrong or doesn't know the piece well. It is quite acceptable to stop and ask to start again. But I feel that it isn't polite to blame the pianist – it is more acceptable to say: "We haven't got the same speed in our heads, maybe I didn't make it clear." You would be surprised how often the panel know when it isn't your fault, but appreciate this courteous way of saying so.

Learning a song – the basics

1) Read the lyrics out loud.

2) Consider the music and lyrics both separately and together. I have noticed that it has become paramount to talk about text, often to the exclusion of the music itself. But we need to make sure we consider both. Always learn the tune accurately – notes AND rhythm. If possible, get the tune recorded very slowly by a good coach. This should be at a speed at which you can think and hear if you're being really accurate. It is much harder to unlearn mistakes than to learn the song correctly to start with. Also, beware of accompaniments where the pianist has tried to be helpful and doubled the tune – you could get a shock at your audition when you hear what the composer really wrote! If you have been fortunate enough to have a learning session with a pianist, always ask for a recording with one slow version with the tune played firmly and clearly, and another in tempo with accompaniment only.

3) Listen to the tune and hear how the composer has set the lyrics. What does the music suggest? Does it influence your understanding?

4) Make sure you aren't copying what you have heard on a cast recording.

5) If you practise by singing along to a recording of another singer, you may find that when it is

taken away you are not using enough energy – it is the singer on the recording that is making the effort, not you. The result is lack-lustre singing. When you practise with a recording that has a rhythmic, instrumental accompaniment (i.e. bass and drums), you will really miss it when you just have a piano accompaniment – unless you've found your own internal rhythm. Ways to do this: walk around the room – or count out loud – in time to the beat (make sure you keep on the beat if the tune is syncopated).

6) For a patter song (i.e. a fast "wordy" song), a good way of learning it is to speak it out loud while doing something else – throwing a cushion in the air, dusting, shopping(!). This will get it into your muscle memory. Some songs go so fast that you don't have time for memory recall so the words have to be automatic.

7) Memorising lyrics: don't try to do too much too quickly. Concentrate on a page at a time. If you find yourself always forgetting the same phrase, try singing the end of the previous phrase into the beginning of the next over and over again to make a connection.

Working on a song

Having chosen your song and started to learn it, how can you go about working on it so that it reflects your personal understanding of the story? How can you use your material to tell the panel something about you as an individual performer? Your voice will shift and change as a result of the decisions you make about the text, so this is the time to put into practice what you've learnt in singing lessons or through experience. The singing voice can express many emotions – anger, pain, frustration, happiness, fear, joy and laughter are just some of them. When singing, the vocal folds have a longer closed phase than is the case for speech – this means that you can hear the changes of vocal colour connected to the emotion behind the thought much more when text is sung.

To integrate acting and singing takes practice. Different voice qualities (whispered intensity, mixed resonance, twang, falsetto, etc.) give life to the meaning of words. You should aim to colour words and sentences to have specific meaning. Your singing voice should convey your exploration of the text from moment to moment – including the active thoughts in the rests and moments of silence – and give the song an individuality reflecting your specific dramatic decisions.

Get on the internet and research the context of the song. It is important to ask yourself whether you need to relate your audition song to the original show/character. Sometimes it is possible to take a song out of context, but much of the time it is worth finding out as much you can about the show, even if you don't always use all the information.

Interpretation

Here are some important questions to ask when preparing your song:

Context

1) Is the character aware of the audience's presence? Can the character address the audience directly? For example, in *Cabaret* or *The Light in the Piazza*, characters "break the fourth wall" and talk to the audience directly.

2) Where is the song set? Is there a specific country or place? If the song is about a place in the character's imagination it is useful to visualise it as being at the back of the stalls or upper circle so that the performance isn't too small and embraces the audience. "What you'd call a dream" from *Diamonds* is an example of this type of song.

3) Accent/dialect. How is this going to affect your voice? Consider how vowel choices will affect your performance. Examples of songs where this is particularly important are "Wick" from *The Secret Garden* and songs from Flahert and Ahrens' *Once on this Island*.

4) Time/era. Be aware that even time of day could affect your vocal choices. For example, "Why God, why?" from *Miss Saigon* (set late at night) might be very different from "Oh what a beautiful mornin'". It is important also to be aware of the historical context of your song (important in, for example, songs from *Rent* or *Camelot*).

5) Age of the character. Does this need to be reflected in your vocal choices? But make sure you don't end up caricaturing the role.

6) Status of the character. Is it upper class, lower class, virtuous, heroic, downtrodden, corrupt . . . ?

7) What has the character experienced earlier in the story?

8) What is going to happen to the character after the song? Does this song affect their journey in any way?

9) What has happened to the character immediately before the song? In other words, what is the IMPETUS to sing? If this isn't clear from the research you've managed to do then you must create your own situation. Careful re-reading of the text of a song you may have known for a long time – even on the way to your audition – helps keep your ideas alive and fresh.

10) Does the song form part of the action of the play? In other words, can the other characters hear it? Examples of this include "Don't tell mama" from *Cabaret* and "Hand me the wine and the dice" from *Aspects of Love*.

11) How does the character express themselves – are they emotional, sexy, confessional? Are they used to expressing themselves in this way? Or is this a first experience (e.g. Freddy in *My Fair Lady* or Bobby in *Company*)?

12) What do you imagine the physical attributes of the character to be?

13) If the character is based on a real-life figure, your characterisation can be informed by historical research (*Evita* and *Assassins* are good examples of this).

Lyrics

1) Do you think this is the first time the character has said these words?

2) Is the character working through a problem in the song? Do they make any decisions? What is the character trying to change (someone else, themselves)?

3) Circle all the linking words ("or", "and", "but", "so") and ALL question marks.

4) Look up any words you don't understand.

5) Are there any repeated lyrics (e.g. "I love him, I love him")? Why are they repeated? Could they express different things?

6) Are there any references to other characters? What is your character's relationship to those mentioned?

7) Go through the lyrics and mark every change of thought.

Music

1) Is the song in a major key or is it minor? Are there any changes of key? How does that influence the mood of the song?

2) How has the composer chosen to pitch the vocal line – is it high, middle or low in the texture? Look for clues to interpretation.

3) Circle every dynamic marking in the score.

4) Is there any repetition of musical material, either from the rest of the show or within the individual song (this is very common in contemporary book musicals)? What might this tell the audience?

5) How are the lyrics set to music? Is the song lyrical or wordy? Why?

6) What is the melodic shape? Smooth, angular, or a mixture of the two? What does this express?

7) Listen to the musical accompaniment on its own. Does it evoke any particular style of

music (e.g. jazz, blues, bluegrass, country and western, rock, pop, classical, folk, patter, Gilbert and Sullivan, torch song, reggae, militant, anthemic . . .)? The accompaniment could suggest what vocal colours, inflections, dynamics and phrasing you need to use.

8) Does the accompaniment do anything sudden or unexpected? e.g. stop, become very quiet or loud? Why do you think the composer has done this?

9) What is the rhythmic identity of the song? Is it swung, straight, regular, irregular? Is the vocal line made up mainly of long or short notes?

In the following section, I have decided to give examples of songs in different styles and show you ways in which you might begin to work on them and make them your own. Giving examples of music in different styles and from different eras is an enormous task. From the wit of Cole Porter, George and Ira Gershwin, Noël Coward and Kander and Ebb, to the subtlety of Sondheim and the romanticism of Boublil and Schönberg and Lloyd Webber, to name but a few: I urge you to explore their writing for yourself. While I have tried to isolate a specific approach for each song, I found that I was constantly cross-referencing each song, as the underlying principles remain the same, whatever the style.

N.B. I have deliberately chosen songs that I would call "classic" – by this I mean material that has withstood the test of time. You will learn most from working on really finely crafted songs with strong lyrics and well-composed music.

"Giants in the Sky" from Into the Woods *by Stephen Sondheim*

Exploring text and music – making choices

I have chosen "Giants in the Sky" by Stephen Sondheim as a good example of a song where the music and lyrics help each other. Even though – as with nearly all Sondheim's music – it is hard to disassociate it from its original context, it will, however, stand on its own as expertly-crafted musical monologue.

The Text

Having chosen this as your audition piece, you need to find out as much as possible about its original context. *Into the Woods* is one of Sondheim's most popular works: in it, he and author James Lapine explore fairy tales we are told as children and expose their darker connotations. One of the stories is Jack's (of beanstalk fame) emotional journey through boyhood to adolescence – slightly darker than the usual pantomime story. Prior to this song, Jack has just sold his cow in exchange for the magic beans and climbs the beanstalk. "Giants in the Sky" is the song he sings on his return to earth.

You need to go through the song line by line – in fact, word by word. First of all, are there any words you don't understand? A thesaurus and dictionary are good companions to your music library. You shouldn't be singing any words you don't understand. Also look at the punctuation, paying particular attention to full stops and commas. Sondheim in particular is meticulous about this, which is really very helpful. For example, he uses exclamation marks in the opening phrases of the song. How can you use these? Are they conveying fear, excitement, the exuberance of youth? These are just a few ideas to get you going.

The giants that Jack sings about in this song could be symbolic of so many things. This is the point at which you as a performer can use your own experiences to inform your choices. Personally, I see the giants as representing the challenges that we have to face as we grow up. Do you agree? What specifically these might be is ultimately up to you. Be brave with your choices.

I like people who are prepared to take a risk with material. It is important for a director to see a creative artist.

Trevor Jackson (casting director)

In terms of considering the original context, you should ask yourself:

- Where has this character been?
- What's he doing now?
- Where's he going?
- Is he working through a problem in the song?
- Does he come to any decisions?
- Who is he talking to? Who is the song for?
- How does he physically reflect his state of mind?
- How old do you think he is?
- How does he feel about his mother?
- What do you think the cow really represents?

This list could go on for pages. The more choices you make, the more detailed your performance will become.

*The audience doesn't need to know what you're thinking, but they do need to know **that** you are thinking*

Hal Prince (director)

A word of warning It is very easy to turn into an amateur psychoanalyst when working on this kind of material –

make sure your choices always serve the text and aren't self-indulgent.

Learning the music

In musical theatre, the above approach to language is essential in creating individual and truthful characterisation. However: DON'T FORGET THE MUSIC! It has become quite usual to focus only on analysing the text without considering the musical content. My plea is that this is **music**al theatre and both need to be considered equally. Don't worry if you don't have musical training (but don't be afraid to use it if you do): what you do need is a good pair of ears and to train yourself to listen. My first approach to this song, before starting to learn the melody, would be to play the accompaniment through (or ask a pianist to play it), to see what ideas it might give you.

Performers rarely seem to understand that any song starts immediately when the pianist (or orchestra) plays the first notes – not just when you begin to sing. In "Giants in the Sky", the first thing we hear is a slightly alarming chord – yet Jack's opening statements are brightly sung in an optimistic nursery-rhyme manner:

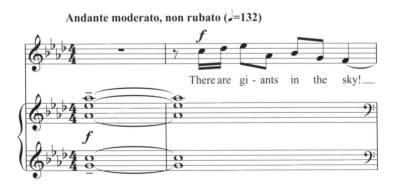

There are big tall ter-ri-ble gi-ants in the sky!

Sondheim has marked this phrase non-rubato (i.e. strict tempo). What is the effect of keeping this music in tempo? I would suggest it avoids sentimentality. What do you think? This is your first decision, the first step to making it *your* song, using what Sondheim has given you. There is something else here to help you make your choices: listen to the chords that underpin Jack's thoughts. Why the change from high up on the piano to the more menacing bass register for the second chord. What does this make you feel?

All of these choices will obviously affect the way you sing these phrases. Are you going to opt for a heavy sound or a light sound? What, for example, do you feel is representative of a nursery rhyme? Should it be loud, soft, breathy? These are all options to consider. The voice quality you choose will suggest much about the character. How old is your Jack? Is he cocky, naïve, overwhelmed? All these are your decisions – to be made after you've thoroughly examined the text and music.

All this is in just the first five bars of music. You'd be surprised how much this tells an audition panel about you as a performer and, if you've done your preparation thoroughly, they'll really want to listen to the rest of the song. Believe me – I've been there!

"One song glory" from Rent *by Jonathan Larson*

A song using rock vocal production in musical theatre

An increasing number of musicals are being written in a rock/pop style: *Grease*, which has a seventies feel, *Footloose*, *Fame* and *We Will Rock You* – all reflect an era and a society which has changed. *Rent* deals with a difficult subject, helping to bring AIDS into public awareness – a brave topic for a musical. Once again, you must know the story – use the internet to find out about it.

Performances of this musical will almost certainly be amplified loudly. However, while the audience will always be able to hear you, you have to ensure that you have done your detailed work, otherwise they will not feel involved dramatically. Making performance choices is sometimes more difficult in a rock style: the songs can seem more formulaic and the accompaniments less obviously connected to the text. This is certainly not a criticism of the style, but a different approach is required. In addition, the driving rhythm of rock and pop can easily carry you along which, while it may feel exciting to sing, does not guarantee a fulfilling experience for the listener. You still need detail and variation in your performance, otherwise you risk getting the dreaded "good rock voice – not an actor" label.

A word of warning Rock songs can be the most difficult to get across with just a piano accompaniment. You have to find your own internal rhythm and be prepared to "drive" the number yourself.

"One song glory" is sung by Roger, who is HIV positive. The composer and author have given him a repetitive idea – the "one song glory" of the title – he wants to leave his mark. He wails with grief at the loss of his girlfriend from the same disease, and his need to find a song that makes sense of life and encapsulates the special love they had. Take a look at the opening phrases:

While the opening guitar riff follows a standard pop-chord progression, what is the effect of the particular motif used? I would suggest it conveys hesitation, restlessness – major and minor keys show fluctuating thoughts, some good, some bad.

Do you agree with that interpretation? Maybe not: it doesn't matter, as long as YOU decide what you want the song to say.

If you look carefully at the music, the way the rests are written could be seen as supporting the character's state of mind. Let's take a close look at what the rhythms do to the language in the opening lines of the song. Written as prose and without punctuation, these phrases seem somewhat abstract and hard to make sense of. It is up to you to decide how to use inflection and silence to make sense of this lyric for your audience. One possible interpretation might be:

> *One song* (. . . of what? . . . response:) *glory* (. . . thinks . . .).
> *One song* (. . . perhaps a plea for recognition . . .)

The repetition of this phrase throughout the song makes it seem like a mantra. Roger's need for just one work of art to make his mark seems somehow elusive. Do you agree? A strong consonant on the final "g" of "song" will propel you forward to the reality of:

> *before I go* (. . . death? . . .)

This is a huge thing to reconcile himself to – particularly as a young man. How will this affect your inflection? Does it scare him? Is he resigned to it?

Glory

Does the repetition of this word carry the same inflection as before? Does it have anger, cynicism, pain, desperation, pleading? All of these have different vocal colours. You should be able to hear a change of thought on just one word.

One song to leave behind

I suggest a crescendo (gradually getting louder), the effect of which is to increase the tension so the word "Find" bursts out of the preceding phrase.

This gives you an idea of the detail needed to make sense of the rhythms in this opening section. Now look at the following musical example:

While the accompaniment remains jagged and restless, the vocal line now features more extended phrases. To me, this is the beginning of a more yearning cry for understanding. Once again, your interpretation will give different voice qualities. From a technical point of view, make sure you have strong consonants on "flies" and "dies", and that you know how many beats are on each word. This will help you avoid using a diphthong (which often makes singers go out of tune) on these words; so "flies" becomes "flaaaa", and "dies" stays as "daaaaaa", until the last beat. A gradual crescendo will keep breath-pressure constant, but don't force.

A note on rock-style singing It is beyond the remit of this book to give detailed explanations of voice production. With the introduction of fibre optics and stroboscopy, we now know much more about safe voice production for rock and pop. However, be wary of using a "pushed-up" chest voice for this style. In an audition, you can often feel tense and end up shouting. In this kind of rock song, the larynx is usually used in a higher position, often with the head tilted backwards (shorter fatter vocal folds) – make sure that you have adequate support with your back and lats muscles and don't overdrive air (forcing). This technique is quite easy to teach, so if you can't find it for yourself, find someone who knows how to help you.

"I don't know how to love him" from **Jesus Christ Superstar** *by Andrew Lloyd Webber*

Exploring context, considering the social and historical background

Let's now think about background, which is a hugely important area. While many of your performance decisions can be based on the words and music of your song, you also need to consider other information. Actors need to think about background and context all the time; singers sometimes forget.

For *Jesus Christ Superstar*, a good place to start is the bible. "I don't know how to love him" is sung by Mary Magdalene. How much do you know about the treatment of women in this era? At times like this, the internet is your best friend and will give valuable information. Mary Magdalene was a prostitute at a time when this meant living outside of society. For her to be treated with respect by Jesus has enormous significance. In my opinion, the love that Jesus has shown is unfamiliar to her and she does not know how to respond. I therefore believe that the song does not need to be overloaded with sexual connotations and should begin very simply.

Here's how I would approach this song if I were preparing for an audition. Obviously, if you were performing it in the context of a show, you would collaborate with the director and musical director in this process. In the meantime, it's up to you.

First of all, look at the rhythms that Lloyd Webber has used. I think the song should be sung exactly as written – see if you agree. In the first phrase, give the word "him" exactly the note-value written. A strong consonant on the "m" gives you a quick intake of breath, which makes sense of the rest preceding the phrase "What to do, how to move him".

In the phrase that follows, the composer has not written a breath before "I've been changed" – it's a thought process that comes directly out of the previous statement, "how to move him". It just doesn't have the same impact if there's a gap before the word "I've" – yet I often hear singers breathe here. Then, if you put a strong consonant on the letter "d" of "changed" it helps the next phrase – "yes really changed" – sound really spontaneous.

Now look at the next two phrases:

On the words "past few" and "seen my-", try to crescendo towards the next syllables ("days" and "-self") in order to avoid what normally comes across, and which doesn't make sense of the phrase:

In these paAAAAAst few days when I've seEEEEEn myself

All of these principles apply to the second part of this verse as well.

Then we get to the most important line – the line that we have been building towards:

This is a really simple line. And yet it isn't. Jesus isn't just one more man. That is why Mary Magdalene is singing this song. This is a heightened moment. Remember when we talked about the background to this song? In a broader sense,

Jesus is both man and God, and Mary Magdalene instinctively understands this. All of this background is contained within "He's just one more". But how do you begin to convey that?

Having sung the song myself and heard it sung thousands of times, I believe you need to give particular emphasis to the consonants in this line. Say the words out loud:

He's just one more.

Feel how the "s" at the end of "He's" elides into the "j" of "just" before opening out to the "u". And how the "n" of "one" hits up against the "m" of "more" – all sung on the one note. All this needs to be done without breaking up the musical line.

If you manage to do all of this, you will achieve exactly the right level of intensity and bring about a complete fusion of words and music. In fact, you will have brought it to life.

Look at the next section:

Should I bring him down?
Should I scream and shout
Should I speak of love
Let my feelings out?
I never thought I'd come to this.
What's it all about?

In this section, don't start too loudly – you have a long way to go. This isn't a song where you want to end up shouting at the audience. Actors sometimes forget that this is an introspective song. Of course, the style of the music changes here – you need to decide why, and how best to make it work. This bridge section is predominantly made up of questions. Who are they directed at? Us? Mary herself? Does she have any of the answers? There are no breaths written into these phrases, so you can choose how to join each individual thought. As mentioned previously, a crescendo on the tied notes gives greater intensity, and strong final consonants on these tied notes kick you forward into the next phrase.

Mary's questions tumble out so quickly that the actress on stage seems not to know which way to move. The first affirmative statement marks the musical climax of the bridge section:

I never thought I'd come to this

And then, yet another question:

What's it all about?

For me, these words convey the very essence of the song. Mary has dealt with being hounded, castigated and despised. She has learned to be hated – how can she now deal with love?

In the last verse, she elucidates the fears she has:

Yet if he said he loved me
I'd be lost I'd be frightened
I couldn't cope…

Notice there is no comma after the word frightened. The next phrase – "I couldn't cope" – is borne directly out of this fear. The final lines clearly reveal her dilemma to us:

I'd turn my head, I'd back away I wouldn't want to know
He scares me so
I want him so
I love him so

What scares her? In my opinion, Jesus represents all the emotions that she's locked away deep inside in order to protect herself – no accident here that we start on a wide open and vulnerable vowel.

The song now repeats. If you choose to sing the repeat in your audition, this is your chance to layer the song further – musically, emotionally or preferably both. Repeating material in auditions is notoriously risky but you may be able to turn it to your advantage.

The 1999 revival of *Jesus Christ Superstar* in the West End had much more of a rock feel than earlier productions, and freer phrasing was used to good effect. A more contemporary approach made Mary seem easier to empathise with – not just a historical figure but a character with relevance to today's society. But if you do this, learn it as written first, bringing in your freer interpretations later.

This is a song of real power and its greatest strength is surely its simplicity. And although it is often performed, I find I have never grown tired of it. Audition panels will gladly listen to well-known material, providing it has individuality and truth.

Choosing a vocal style

Many singers will be wondering what voice quality to use. However, to suggest that you should sing a particular song with a specific voice quality is, I feel, prescriptive and therefore wrong. All I would say is that your detailed work on background and musical "close-reading" will put you in a far better position to make judgements about voice quality for yourself.

A note on "belting"

Many people approach sections of this song as a chance to show off their "belt" voice in an audition. This is a powerful vocal sound and you should only use it if it relates to the text and adds to the meaning. It communicates intense emotion and requires a very high level of physicality. When the right conditions are maintained, both in the larynx and the body, it is a safe and exciting quality that is free from strain. It must not be mistaken for chest voice taken high. Belting should always be an expression of great emotion – never simply used for its own sake.

"Anything goes" from Anything Goes *by Cole Porter*

Rhythm serving the lyrics

Anything Goes is an example of a much earlier style of musical theatre. It was a hit in the thirties and has been revived many times, including a recent Trevor Nunn production at the National Theatre and in the West End. I want to use this song to illustrate how important it is to learn rhythms accurately. Cole Porter wrote his own lyrics and music and you should aim to start by singing exactly what he wrote before adapting anything. In this style, the musical director will want you to come to the audition with your own interpretation – but without distorting the music. In particular, back-phrasing (i.e. singing behind the beat) has to be tasteful rather than the result of inaccurate learning. Be warned – the panel will know the difference!

People often leave out the verses of these older songs and yet I think they are often really useful in an audition as they give you the opportunity to communicate directly with the panel in a way that a refrain doesn't always allow. "Anything goes" is a great example of this; the opening phrase is a very strong statement which allows you to grab the audience's attention:

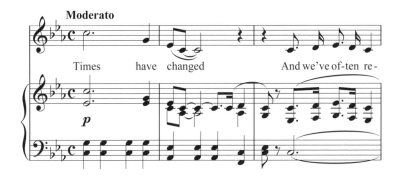

Come in on the opening beat with a strong "T" and really show them your voice. You've got a full three beats to tell the panel that you are right for the job. What a useful contrast, after that bold lyrical opening, then to use the jazzy dotted rhythms of the next three phrases. Be true to this rhythm and see how effective it can be and how clear the story becomes.

Porter takes delight in complex rhymes – distort the phrase and you won't reap the full benefit of his rhyme scheme. Look at the words and rhythmic placing of "clock", "shock" and "rock" – if you sing the rhythm as written it lands the puns right in your lap! This is where the work you have done on the muscles of your mouth and tongue pays dividends. Strong consonants with co-ordination exactly on the beat make the words have real impact without forcing – you don't have to do any more than sing what's there. Trust clever writing – you probably won't improve on it – and, once again, learn accurately.

Another of Cole Porter's trademarks is his clever use of syncopation – emphasising offbeats. Think of songs such as "Blow Gabriel, blow" and "You're the top". And look at the refrain of "Anything goes":

When Porter writes about "stocking" and "something shocking", he uses syncopated rhythms that seem to match the naughtiness of his thought – contrasting with the straight crotchets on either side. See how the rhythms give us our interpretation – Porter has already done the work for you.

You could have fun with the song by trying a number of different accents. As well as the standard American, look what a pompous English accent does to the lyrics. Try French, Scottish – anything you like which suits the audition. Be imaginative!

"If I loved you" from Carousel *by Rodgers and Hammerstein and "The sun whose rays are all ablaze" from* The Mikado *by Gilbert and Sullivan*

Songs using more "legit" vocal production in musical theatre

Very often, your agent may call you with a request for a more "legit" song. This means a song with a light classical sound and natural-sounding vowels. Shows that might need this are cross-over shows like *The Merry Widow, Hot Mikado, Jerry Springer: The Opera* or a rep season which includes some light operetta.

Vocal line and text

Anyone who teaches singing would say that consistent airflow is really important. It is our "bowing arm" (i.e. if a violinist doesn't have control of the bow then nothing that is done with the left hand registers). Without a steady stream of air passing through the vocal folds we have little chance of communicating the language. (This is most often called "support" but I prefer the words breath management or airflow.) However, as I have re-iterated throughout this book, musical theatre is the marriage of music and text. A beautiful vocal line is all very well but, in the theatre, our job is to tell stories.

"If I loved you" from Rodgers and Hammerstein's *Carousel* is one of the great songs in the musical-theatre canon. The difficulty with such a sweeping expansive melody is to do justice to the music while being specific with the text. If you emphasise too many words it disturbs the flow of the melody, but if just the melody comes across, the comment in auditions will be that it is too "sung"! This is a very common criticism; it means that the panel can't hear the detail in the text. It is possible to achieve both – to have a lovely sound that conveys character and meaning. With the short extract below I hope you'll be able to see how you can be very specific with your acting choices while honouring the musical requirements of "legit" singing.

In the original show, Billy and Julie sing this number as a duet. It is now more often published as a solo song, but it is worth looking at the original setting.

Look at the opening phrase:

Does it give you a choice as to the most important word? Mostly singers work towards the word "loved", so we get:

If I LOVED *you*

To emphasise this, you need a strong "l" and "d" to mark the intensity of the feeling, but make sure you have a long vowel between the two.

What are your other options, though? I suggest you look at what happens if you play around with the phrase. For example

If **I** *loved* **YOU**

See how differently this expresses the same phrase. In this case, be careful not to slide on the "y" of "you" – this could make it sound over-sentimental.

Now try this:

IF *I loved you*

Start this with a soft glottal – often thought of as dangerous. It is important to have the vocal control to do this as the English language is full of glottal stops and in musical theatre they are used all the time. Always make sure they are soft glottal stops – never hard.

All of these versions say different things. My personal preference is for the last one, which is more teasing or flirty. This is possibly what was intended by Richard Rodgers – neither Julie or Billy are used to being romantic and they are finding it hard to directly say what they feel.

Another idea about phrasing: avoid only stressing lyrics that fall on a strong beat. I love the outpouring of "Time and again I would try to say all I'd want you to know". The tune lands on the word "try", but ensure that you give equal emphasis to the phrase as a whole. Many singers break the phrase after the word "say", which doesn't make sense of the line. It is perfectly possible to take a breath but continue the thought. This is a very important point – always think through breaths and connect them to the next thought. With good control of airflow, you have a chance to express yourself in many different ways.

This illustrates how much detail can be found in just a few lines. But I would emphasise the importance of good technical ability. Long vowels and strong consonants fulfil the level of detail demanded by this style – so back to the scales and tongue-twisters! It's always easier to practise when you know how it relates to your craft.

Vowel modification in musical theatre

"Classical" voice production gives you strong muscularity and is good grounding for any style of singing. It does, however, need to be adapted for musical theatre, which doesn't demand such "round" vowel sounds. In musical theatre, vowels are often modified and occasionally diphthongs are embraced. As I have just mentioned, soft glottal stops are also used: something not necessarily encouraged in classical singing.

I will use Yum Yum's song "The sun whose rays are all ablaze" from *The Mikado* as an example. For the purposes of musical theatre, this song should have a strong vocal line – as written, but keeping the vowels as natural-sounding as possible (many of the thoughts in the section on "If I loved you" apply also to this song). I would say that this style of song benefits from a lighter sound than would be usual in classical-singing voice production. However, this depends on the individual singer and their training.

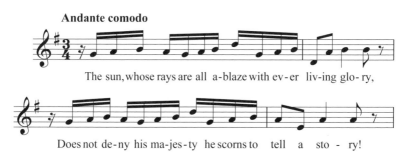

He won't ex- claim,"I blush for shame,so kind-ly be in-dul- gent;"

But,fierce and bold,in fie-ry gold,he glo-ries all ef - ful - gent!

Speak the words first, then try singing while keeping the shape of the vowels as close as possible to that of speech. This won't/ can't sound exactly like an extension of speech but it will help you find the shapes needed to make your voice as natural as possible. I would always advocate recording yourself – it won't give you an accurate representation of tonal quality but is a good guide to hearing unnatural vowel sounds. Practise short phrases and give yourself time to think. Be aware that, if you have been classically trained, your voice will almost automatically find shapes it is used to.

In the first few phrases, watch out for "blaze", "tell", "exclaim", "shame" and any vowels that sound "precious". Experiment, and find a more natural vowel.

Questions to ask yourself:

- Is your tongue relaxed?
- Is your jaw loose?
- Is the airflow free?

Now let's take the phrase "We really know our worth":

Andante comodo

We real - ly know our worth, __ The sun and I!

The word "know" is the clue to climbing up to "our worth". Make sure the word "know" is *tilted*. Other descriptions for this, which may resonate with you and mean the same thing, are "think forward", "think through the eyes" and "think higher and brighter". In technical terms, what we want is the larynx to tilt forward with a contraction of the crico-thyroid muscle so that the vocal folds lengthen and the larynx is helped to perform the gymnastics required to sing "our worth" – it is very difficult to sing a "w" consonant so high. Is it any wonder that the audience often can't understand a word when we sing so high? Musical theatre doesn't permit unintelligibility, so practise "our worth" without a diphthong on "our" – this gives "AAH worth", which is just about acceptable – and keep the air pressure consistent for "worth". Keep practising and you'll find your tongue will make adjustments to accommodate this higher position.

Textbooks on voice and singing are useful but cannot replace attentive listening and knowing what to listen for. If this all seems too technical then a few sessions with someone with an experienced ear can help. Singing teachers have their uses!

"Goodnight Saigon" by Billy Joel

Making a pop-song lyric work for theatre

For shows demanding a contemporary sound, it can be useful to look at well-crafted pop songs. Writers such as Elton John, Billy Joel, Stevie Wonder, George Michael, Bruce Springsteen, Nora Jones, Dusty Springfield, Kate Bush and Gloria Estefan have stood the test of time and are worth exploring. Also, consider any songs that speak to you personally. If you believe in the story, you will find your own truth and that will come through in your voice.

What is meant by a "contemporary sound"? There are many components to this – a light sound, natural vowels, soft glottal stops, the larynx often neutral (speech quality) or allowed to rise as necessary.

I found "Goodnight Saigon" when I was looking for an audition song for the role of Chris in *Miss Saigon*. Apart from the coincidence of title, I found the lyrics expressive of Chris's emotional journey in the show. I spent ten years working on *Miss Saigon*, and the plight of young soldiers drafted unknowingly into Vietnam always touched me. Sometimes you can trust your gut reaction to a piece of music – which was what happened for me here. The song has the disjointedness of someone thinking through their experiences and a suggestion of inner torment. If you find a song which resonates with the character for which you are auditioning, it can really help the panel see you in that role without actually using music from the show.

In the first sentence of the song, we hear a man enjoying his friends and feeling a spirit of camaraderie: "We met as soul mates". But immediately the second phrase, "We left as inmates", tells us what actually happens as a result of his experience. These lyrics work effectively with a very naturalistic sound. You don't want to be over dramatic; the emotional core of the song is strong enough. Keep to the written rhythms; the gaps in the music don't need to be breaths but just suggest disjointed thoughts.

The next phrase is, "And we were sharp, sharp as knives and we were so gung-ho to lay down our lives". For audition purposes, apart from the lovely simplicity of the tune, the music begins to show the vocal range of the character and it is possible to use a more "pop" sound. For English singers, to sing with an American accent use an open "Aah" and a soft rolled "R" (this accent is often called "mid-Atlantic") – this will avoid caricaturing the language. For example: *"Aaand we werrrre shaaaarrrrrp"*. This looks ridiculous written out, but try it. Sing the above phrase in both an English and an American accent. How does it feel different? In American, your larynx will rise so the top notes become much easier to achieve. Also, an American accent always adds an additional resonance, commonly known as twang, which carries well, even when singing quietly.

Vocal Preparation

One of the keys to a good audition is getting your voice warmed up – i.e. making sure the blood supply is going to the necessary places. To be able to sing at your best after a journey, possibly having had a long wait – and while coping with nerves – has to be planned carefully. It is also helpful to see a singing teacher from time to time and have some vocal exercises tailored to your particular voice. Ten minutes of exercise twice a day will make a significant difference to your range and stamina.

> *When casting for a year and performing eight shows a week, I like to see performers with a strong instrument – I value a strong vocal ability!*

Trevor Jackson (casting director)

Preparing at home the night before

Don't over-practise your material! Over-practising is very common and completely understandable. If it is a first audition, I would suggest you choose a song you know reasonably well. Before you sing it through, re-read the text and recommit to the sense of it – especially if you've known it for a while. "Acting through the song" can only happen if you have made decisions about the song's dramatic journey. Your voice should be able to express that journey – so knowing *what* story you want to tell is paramount.

You should try to get a recording of the piano accompaniment to work to. Although this has the disadvantage of making you always practise at the same speed, it is certainly useful for practising.

If you do a thorough warm-up the night before, it shouldn't be necessary to wear yourself out by doing too much on the day of the audition. If you actually sing regularly, you should find you warm up quite quickly. It is mainly getting the body going in the morning that counts.

The warm-up CD

I have recorded some exercises, both physical and vocal, to help you warm up – that is, to get blood flowing easily to the relevant muscles.

Track listing:

1) Introduction
2) Physical exercises
3) Face and neck muscles
4) Breathing naturally
5) Linking breath to the singing voice
6) Sliding exercise
7) Descending scale
8) Sirening
9) Humming
10) Exercises using "oo"
11) Adding more vowels
12) Extended patterns
13) Light, flexible exercises
14) Strong, driving rhythm
15) Brain and tongue
16) *Bella Signora*
17) Conclusion

CD warm-ups section

CD track 2: physical exercises

Any vocal warm-up should start with a short physical warm-up:

Gentle head rolls

This exercise is to stretch the strong muscles of the neck and to release tension.

1) Gently drop your head on your chest and let the weight of your head stretch the muscles of the neck.

2) Starting from this position, slowly roll your head around until your right ear is close to your right shoulder.

3) Looking upwards, you should feel your spine elongating. Keep breathing and relax your jaw. Don't drop your head all the way back – this will stress your neck muscles.

4) Continue the head-roll and circle until your left ear is near your shoulder. This should be a continuous slow movement, rolling your head through each of these positions. If you feel tension in a particular spot just let the weight of your head naturally stretch out that muscle.

Do this exercise a few times then reverse the direction.

Shoulder rolls

This exercise should release tension in the upper back and shoulders. Auditions can make us carry more tension in our shoulders than normal. Stretching them will help release tension that could inhibit free vocal production.

1) Bring both shoulders up to your ears, then roll them back so that it feels like your shoulder blades are almost touching.

2) Release your shoulders into a relaxed position and then bring them forward so your upper body feels rounded.

3) Reverse this exercise in a continuous movement.

You may now feel literally warmer as your muscles have oxygen pumped round them. Remember to breathe normally throughout all these exercises.

Rib stretches

This exercise will help your breathing and can also relieve tension.

1) Stand with your feet apart – the width of your shoulders is usually comfortable.

2) Reach up to the ceiling (palm upwards) with your right arm, bend your right knee a little, keeping the left leg straight.

3) Stretch your right arm above your head and lean slightly to your left.

4) Reverse this – you should feel a good stretch in your rib muscles.

Rolling down

This exercise stretches your back, legs and muscles that hold you upright. When you bend over, *always* do just what is comfortable. Don't push yourself! Remember – on the day of the audition, you are just preparing yourself – not trying anything new. Be very careful not to lock your knees.

CD warm-ups section

85

1) Stand with your feet slightly apart, level with your hips. Slowly drop your chin on to your chest and, leading with your head, continue to roll down – one vertebra at a time – until you are bending over at the waist.

2) Take a deep breath – feel your ribs expand and let go of your belly. Keep your head and neck relaxed.

3) Keeping this position, keep breathing deeply and stretch your legs a few times by strengthening the knees.

4) Lean back slightly – make sure your hips are over your feet – push your feet on the floor and straighten up, one vertebra at a time. Use your legs to do this rather than your back.

CD track 3: face and neck muscles

To get your face muscles working, you can chew – pretend you have a large piece of bubblegum in your mouth. Walk around the room at the same time.

Massage your neck, facial muscles and jaw

1) Sitting in a relaxed position, massage the back and sides of your neck with your fingers.

2) Work your fingers from the muscles in front of your ears down around the jaw line.

3) Relax your mouth, place your thumb directly under your chin – where it feels quite soft – and massage gently.

4) Work your way up the back of your neck and massage your scalp.

5) Finish with firm finger strokes from the inside corner of your eyebrows to the outside corner.

This physical preparation looks a lot when you write it down but should take less than five minutes in practice.

Breathing

A good warm-up to get your breathing going is to put one hand under your sternum – give a little cough and you will feel the muscle jump. Using your other hand, put your thumb on your belly button and stretch the fingers over your abdominal wall. (That's not the same as your stomach, which contains food and is a little higher up!)

Using a "sh" or "sss" sound, gradually expel all the air until you are empty – then just let the muscles release. When you breathe in, your diaphragm will descend and flatten out – which makes more room for your lungs to expand. When you breathe out, your diaphragm relaxes back up.

Now breathe in. Your abdomen will go out. Breathe out – abdomen in. Once you've got this recoil system going, you can use it to make sound.

Vocal warm-ups

There are many variations of simple warming-up exercises. I mainly use "good old Italian techniques" using the vowel "ee", which helps the vocal folds come together. If you aren't used to this and find it causes constriction (usually via your tongue), try the same exercise with your tongue sticking out. If this doesn't help, go back to the "ah" vowel – if that is what you are more used to. However, I suggest that you aim to try and find the right position for your tongue to sing "ee" comfortably.

CD warm-ups section

Humming, sliding and lip trills are all good for getting the blood flow to your vocal folds – which is the whole purpose of warming up. Lip trills – practise these evenly – really connect to your body as you create continuous air pressure to make the sound. If you find these difficult, use "zzz" or "vvv". Some people find it helps to lip trill if you put an index finger at each corner of your mouth.

CD track 4: breathing naturally

This is an exercise to get your breath flowing. Put one foot in front of the other and your thumb on your belly button. Stretch your hand down and that will help locate the abdominal muscles that are involved with the diaphragm. Rock forwards with a slightly open mouth, taking a breath in. As you rock backwards, exhale with a gentle push on the abdominal wall (belly) to help locate the relevant muscles and remind them to work. Repeat this. Now make the following sounds on the out-breath as you rock backwards.

"sss . . . sss . . . sss"
"shh . . . shh . . . shh"
"fff . . . fff . . . fff"

Repeat these sounds in a rhythmic pattern and feel your breath and body working.

CD track 5: linking breath to the singing voice

If you make any of the following sounds you will feel breath vibrating against your mouth – they are "fricatives" (resistant to breath) and you will feel your body responding.

"vvv"
"zzz"
"jjj"

Choose one of the above and then do the following exercise:

CD track 6: sliding exercise

This is the same as the previous exercise, but uses an "e" vowel. This vowel helps close the vocal folds, but make sure you don't use a hard attack – think of saying the word "eat". This is called a soft glottal. It is essential to keep your tongue relaxed in this exercise. However, if you aren't used to this and find it causes constriction (usually in the tongue), try it with your tongue sticking out. You won't make a nice sound, but it can help you feel where any tongue-root tension might be.

If this isn't helpful, go back to the "ah" vowel – if that is what you are more used to. However, I would suggest that you aim to try and find the right position for your tongue to make the "ee" sound comfortably.

CD track 7: descending scale

Start by using the vowel "e"

Then repeat it using, "ah", "eh" and "aw".

Always sing with a sense of musical phrasing – it helps your breath flow.

None of these exercises I have described so far is particularly high – they are just to warm up, without going to extremes.

CD track 8: sirening

Sirening is a way of letting your larynx go up and down and stretching the vocal folds without putting any pressure on them. Start by saying the word "sing". The back of your tongue and soft palate will touch if the tongue is raised at the back and spread on the sides – probably touching the top back molars. The tip remains at the front, either behind your bottom teeth or loosely in front.

Using your tongue and soft palate, make a small whining or mewing sound like a cat. Keep it very quiet – you may feel like the sound is coming down your nose (you will find it easier if you don't use much breath).

Start in the middle of your range with a very small sound and go up and down a few notes – still making the "ng" sound – and gradually extend either side. It's fine to hear the changes of register; these will be smoother if you don't tense and constrict your larynx. You might sound as if you are yodeling at first, until you get used to it.

Walk around sirening up and down, using the whole of your range. Don't be tempted to force – keep the space small. Roll your shoulders, get your body moving – feel the sound connected to all of your body. You can do sirening silently. Try it; you will feel the larynx going up and down and the muscles that help lift it up and down being used – useful in a shared flat at 6.30 on the morning of the audition.

CD track 9: humming

Say the word "nummm": feel how your tongue releases. You should feel the sounds vibrating – in a relaxed way – against your teeth and lips. Walk around, relax your body as well.

CD track 10: exercises using "oo"

If you put your forefinger in your mouth and close your lips around it, it will alter your tongue position and help find the shape to make the right sound. Try the following exercise:

CD track 11: adding more vowels

This exercise helps to keep a steady stream of air flowing – use the vowels "ee", "eh" and "ah":

CD warm-ups section

CD track 12: extended patterns

This isn't very different from the previous exercise, but extends the pattern. Again using the vowels "ee", "eh" and "ah", keep the breath flowing gently – don't force it or "blow air". If you force breath, it has the effect of blowing the vocal folds apart. You need to aim to create sufficient air pressure to maintain a steady stream of air so that the vocal folds vibrate efficiently.

CD track 13: light, flexible exercises

Sing the following exercise very lightly but don't let breath escape:

CD track 14: strong, driving rhythm

This exercise uses "meh". Sing with a strong, driving rhythm and feel your body work – but don't force.

MEH MEH MEH MEH MEH MEH MEH MEH MEH MEH

ETC.

MEH MEH MEH MEH MEH MEH MEH MEH MEH MEH

CD track 15: brain and tongue

This exercise gets both your brain and your tongue working and co-ordinating:

TICK TACK TICK - Y TICK - Y TICK TACK TICK - Y TICK - Y

TICK TACK TICK - Y TICK - Y TICK TACK TICK - Y TICK - Y

TICK - Y TICK - Y TICK - Y TICK - Y TACK - Y TACK - Y TACK - Y TACK - Y

ETC

TICK-Y TICK-Y TICK-Y TICK-Y TACK-Y TACK-Y TACK-Y TACK-Y   TICK TACK

CD track 16: "Bella Signora!"

This is an exercise which gives a sense of performance. Much used and loved by West-End musical directors and performers, it helps you enjoy the freedom of singing. Walk around the room, throw cushions in the air – anything that encourages a feeling of release.

These simple warm-up exercises just give an idea of what you can use. However, don't confuse warming-up with a vocal workout – you can very easily do too much. In particular, if you have a rock or pop audition I suggest that after you have done a selection of these (or similar) exercises, then the most useful thing would be to sing through a pop song that you know very well or are comfortable with – although not necessarily the one you are planning to sing in the audition.

"My voice doesn't feel right – should I audition tomorrow?"

This is a difficult question to answer. To be frank, nerves can often convince you that you are more ill than you really are. If a student telephones me to ask the above question I sometimes say, "Imagine you are going on holiday – how would you feel then?" Sometimes the answer is "I wouldn't go," sometimes the answer is, "you're right, I'm not *that* bad."

If you have a bad cold, it doesn't always affect your vocal folds, although it can make you feel really unwell. But often it will dehydrate you, so the answer is to inhale steam. Avoid the medicines that say they will clear up your cold – they will also dry up your throat. The best remedy is an early night.

A word of caution, if it hurts to sing: don't sing. You can often sing over a cold if you have nasal congestion but no throat symptoms. This could result in a bit of nasality in the tone, but you can sing through this. However, keep the mucus in your vocal tracts thin by drinking lots of water. Inhaling steam is helpful.

In the morning, if you still feel your voice is hoarse or not functioning, try stretching and getting your body working. Run on the spot for a minute and then try to siren or do gentle exercise. Don't be tempted to force. If your voice isn't responding after maybe three minutes of the first or second exercises, then you have to decide whether to cancel the audition. This is a really difficult decision if you've been waiting a long time for an opportunity to show your talent – sometimes there are long gaps between auditions and they are very precious. However, managements are mostly understanding and will try to fit you in another time. Even if they can't, don't waste your time – or theirs – by giving a lot of excuses when you get to your audition. It doesn't work and it would be better if you simply weren't there.

If you have an agent, they will be able to sort this out for you. If you don't, try to ring the theatre stage door and get a message to the stage-manager.

Things to do the night before

- Do a good warm-up and stop practising by early evening.

- Don't worry if you don't feel relaxed enough to sleep – put on a mindless DVD or video and try to let your body relax.

- Possibly go for a swim or a gentle gym session. It's OK to circuit-train but be careful how you lift weights. Don't strain your vocal mechanism.

- Avoid spicy foods.

Things not to do the night before

- Don't stay out late in a smoky atmosphere – this can really dry your throat.

- Don't go for a long journey in a car and talk or sing over the radio. The background noise of the engine makes you speak and sing louder to hear yourself – if a journey is unavoidable, bear this in mind.

- Don't take any drug to "relax" you – it will also relax the muscles needed to make sound and your voice could sound much lower in the morning.

- Don't get a meal late at night – often the cause of acid reflux, especially if you are nervous. Lots of research has been done and this is often found to be the cause of unexpected hoarseness the next day.

- Don't let nerves make you over-practise. It is not the time to think, "I'm determined to sing the song in the original key with an impressive high note that I can't usually get."

Preparation on the audition day

If you have an early audition – for example 10am – get up early (you'll feel dreadful by midday but at least you'll feel good for the audition). I suggest you get up at 7am at the latest.

1) Do at least ten minutes gentle stretching and physical exercise.

2) Hum gently and then start sirening mid-range – don't stretch yourself.

3) Drink water or herbal tea (except peppermint) rather than caffeine (tea or coffee), which dehydrates you and can make you jittery. If you can't face the day without a coffee, try decaffeinated – maybe not ideal, but it might fool you just this once.

4) Keep sirening and do some sliding exercises – none of these are too loud and are ideal if you have a neighbour problem.

5) Have a shower – if possible. Let the bathroom get REALLY steamy – it's good for the voice.

6) **Eat a good breakfast**. A car needs petrol to run – you need food. Even if you are really nervous, eat something you know you can digest – porridge is good and will give you energy for some time.

7) Do about five to ten minutes of vocal exercises, if you can – choose exercises you find most helpful. It will really help your voice if you've done a physical warm-up first, even if you aren't going to dance. Performers often mistake "my voice doesn't feel warmed-up" for having not warmed up their whole body. If you live

somewhere where you can't make noise, or it's too early in the morning, the CD includes ideas of how to warm up with as little noise as possible.

For waking up your body first thing in the morning, a good exercise is to slap yourself quite firmly! Start at the left shoulder and slap all the way to your right hip (following the line of an imaginary seat belt), then reverse the process using your left hand. Bend over and, using both hands, slap all the way down your legs and, after slapping the back of your legs, try to reach your waist area. Next, use your left hand all the way down your right arm and then do the opposite with your right hand. This sounds a bit weird, but I'm often introduced to ideas like this at voice conferences – they are intended to wake up your "chakras" or source of energy. This one made me smile when I was introduced to it but, to my surprise, I found it made me feel much better.

On the way to the audition

Practise singing exercises to your walking rhythm – this is a good idea to keep your voice working when on the move. Sirening won't disturb people – perhaps even try it silently on the tube. Refer to the CD for suggestions of what you can try.

At the audition

It is often difficult to keep warming-up at the audition venue, as there will be a lot of people around. But you can still:

1) Siren.

2) Do breathing exercises, releasing your diaphragm.

3) Try some of the physical exercises suggested on the CD.

4) Keep slightly moving on the spot while waiting – this keeps your adrenaline pumping.

5) Concentrate on your song – in your mind, focus on what you will be singing. Keep the ideas right in the forefront of your mind.

Speaking voice

So far, we have concentrated only on your singing voice. However, your speaking voice can tell the panel a lot about you and, in the case of a book musical or rep season, you have to be able to perform dialogue as well as your sung material. You should try to have at least a couple of sessions with a spoken-word vocal coach.

Watch your posture in daily life – some habits (e.g. a collapsed back or ribs and an extended neck) can put unnecessary strain on your larynx.

Find a comfortable, connected way of speaking. Have you adopted:

1) A too-low (pseudo sexy!) speaking voice?

2) A too-high (little girl or immature boy) speaking voice?

Avoid shouting at sports matches. This is easy to forget, but it puts pressure on your vocal folds and makes them swell up. The only way they will go back down to normal is if you are silent – not helpful if you have an audition.

Avoid talking over loud music at a gig or party – perhaps go outside for a chat if you don't want to be antisocial. Choose restaurants or cafés that don't have loud music. You'd be surprised to find how loudly you are talking if the music were switched off.

Don't smoke. I can't prescribe how you live your life, but cigarette smoke and its effects are well-documented. It's not helpful either to you or your career. Recreational drugs affect your chemical balance. If singing is your chosen career, it is best to avoid all inhaled substances.

Too much alcohol can cause difficulties with your sense of pitch and it coats the mucus membranes that line the throat and larynx. Heavy drinking and singing are not compatible.

Some factors that contribute to a dry throat and hoarseness

- Too much practice, particularly loud practice.
- Central heating – especially underfloor. Make sure you have damp towels on the radiators or a bowl of water by your bed. You can buy a dehumidifier.
- Hay-fever sufferers should be aware of the effect of antihistamines that dry your throat.
- Aspirin should not be used for gargling.
- Habitually clearing your throat – often an effect of nerves – leads to dehydration.
- Talking over car-engine noise.
- Air travel.

Acid reflux – a burning sensation in your throat – can also lead to hoarseness. A simple explanation of acid reflux is that acid produced to digest your food washes over your vocal folds. You can get advice from a doctor – who will normally give you a lacto-acid product to neutralise the acid. To lessen the possibility of acid reflux:

- Avoid eating spicy food.

- Avoid eating late at night.
- Try sleeping with your head at a higher level than your feet.

The audition

This section provides a rough outline of what to expect at a first-round singing audition and will be particularly useful for those who don't have much experience. It will serve equally well as a handy checklist/reminder for the "well-seasoned" performer.

The night before

- Make sure you feel comfortable and confident in whatever you have chosen to wear – it saves a lot of agonising in the morning. Is there any chance that you will be called back to dance and, if so, do you have a suitable change of clothes and shoes with you?

- Check that your music is taped together or put in a folder with the pages in the correct order and clearly marked up. If you have a particularly long song then a folder is preferable – this reduces the risk of the music cascading to the floor during your big moment. If you are using a complete score, make sure you have marked the correct page and, if you have bought a new book for your audition, you should – heart-breaking though it is – break the spine to stop it snapping shut on the poor pianist, mid-song.

- Double-check the time and venue and plan your journey.

- Now is not the time to have a row with your partner – deal with it later!

- Eat well and, no matter how tempting a relaxing glass or two of wine may seem, remember that alcohol dehydrates you – it's not worth the dry mouth the next day!

Your audition bag

Things to take with you:

- *Personal stereo/MP3 player* If you have managed to record the accompaniment to your song(s) then take this along and listen to it on the bus or tube. If you are at all unsure of how fast your song should go – and adrenaline can do bizarre things to your sense of tempo – don't be afraid to have a quick listen just before you go into the audition room. Try walking in the correct tempo so it gets into your body.

- *CV and headshot* In most cases, your agent will have sent these to the casting director in advance or they may already have been downloaded off the web. However, it is always a good idea to have a couple of spares in your bag, just in case.

- *Music folder* Though you will probably have prepared one or two songs specifically for your audition, it is crucial to take along your repertoire folder in case the panel feel that they need to hear something different.

- *Big bottle of water* Fear can make your mouth go dry.

- *A to Z or map* Even if you think you know where you are going, transport disasters might mean you need to change your route.

Getting there

Audition venues vary enormously, from the less glamorous church halls to fully-fledged rehearsal studios or the theatre itself. If you are auditioning at a venue unknown to you, it is sometimes a good idea to check it out the day before so you can make your way there without any fuss on your audition day. A sneak preview of the actual space you are auditioning in can also be useful – its size and layout will affect the size of your own performance.

- Allow plenty of time for the journey so you don't add any unnecessary stress to what may already be a nervy day.

- If you are driving, try to find out about parking in advance.

- Remember, if all else fails (particularly in big cities), get a cab – they can drive in bus lanes.

Use your journey to re-read the lyrics, ask yourself why you have chosen these songs and make sure you are clear about what you want to show the panel. Even if you are on the train or bus, you can still use the time to warm up your voice. Sirening is a good way of getting your voice working without disturbing fellow travellers – see page 90 for some exercises to try.

N.B. If you have woken up on the morning of your audition with very little voice, you can try inhaling steam or drinking warm water. If your voice is not responding after sirening gently and trying the sliding exercises on the warm-up CD (gently), you may have to consider rescheduling your audition. This should be a last resort, but you should not sing when you have an infection.

When you arrive

You will usually be greeted by a member of stage-management who will tick your name off a list of what may seem like a thousand other candidates. Check if they are running to schedule so you have a rough idea of when you will be seen. Depending on the type of audition, you may well find yourself in a waiting area full of nervous actors. If possible, try to find a quiet spot where you can focus on your pieces and avoid the showbiz gossip that may be flying back and forth (remember that people show nerves in a variety of ways). The important thing is not to be distracted from the real reason you are there. If you are worried about appearing 'stand-offish', have a phrase up your sleeve like "I'm sorry, but I just need to go through the words to my songs for a moment".

Now you have arrived, **switch off your mobile!**

Be prepared for auditions running late – try not to give yourself the stress of having to catch a particular train or get back to work by a certain time. Equally, be prepared for the auditions to run early – if another candidate doesn't turn up or if they are running ahead of schedule, you may well be asked to go in as soon as you arrive (this is a good reason to warm-up your voice en route). If this happens, don't be afraid to ask for five minutes to nip to the loo and get your thoughts together first.

If you are within earshot of the auditions, try not to become paranoid/over-analytical. You will often hear horror stories of actors hearing their song being belted brilliantly by the candidate before them. Apart from perhaps serving as a good warning against choosing obvious audition material, remember that the panel will be interested in your interpretation of your song.

Even though you've not yet entered the room, don't forget that the way you interact with the stage-management can really work to your advantage. As well as finding good performers, the creative team will want a company of people who are pleasant to be around.

Entering the room

As you enter the audition room, a member of stage-management will introduce you to the panel (usually seated behind a table), who may introduce themselves to you in turn. All panels want to put you at your ease – some are better at it than others.

A note on body language: your state of mind can be reflected in your posture. No one wants to look arrogant and it is a fine line between that and looking confident. However, an apologetic, hunched appearance won't fill the panel with confidence. Practise holding yourself well and make the panel feel at ease with *you*.

Don't be put off if the panel are munching sandwiches or drinking coffee: audition days can be very long and without a break, so lunch can often be an ongoing affair. At this point, they may wish to hear you sing straight away, but also be prepared to chat first – they may want to talk to you about the project you are auditioning for or ask you about work on your CV, where you trained, etc. Think about this before you go. When it is time to sing, it is good if you can offer a choice of material and ask what would be most useful for them to hear (more often than not, the panel will then tell you to choose whichever song it is you feel most comfortable with).

Don't waffle! You will probably be a little nervous but try to stop yourself from rambling – listen carefully to any questions asked and take your time to answer them.

Don't apologise for your performance in advance. The panel need to see someone who they feel they could enjoy in a rehearsal situation and trust in performance.

When talking about previous work, do try and be positive and proud of your achievements, be they West-End runs or drama-school projects.

Your performance

Having decided which song you should sing, hand over your music/folder/book to the pianist and take your time to explain carefully any repeats or special markings in the music and make sure they are aware of changes of tempo. Often, the easiest way to help the pianist (who may well be playing your chosen song for the very first time) is to sing the first line or two to them – not only does this give the tempo but it can also swiftly indicate the overall style you are after. See *How to help the pianist* on page 46 for more on this.

Once this is done, make your way to the centre of the space: not too far away from the panel but not singing directly into their faces – this will obviously depend on the venue. If you've already said what you are going to sing, don't feel the need to reiterate it before you start. However, if you've not yet announced your choice you may want to do so now, along with either the name of the composer or the show it comes from. Usually, the pianist will give you time to get settled and wait for an acknowledgement before starting the intro – just a thank you and a smile will do. Although this may sound over-prescriptive, small points like this can really make it appear that you are in control of your performance and make a favourable impression.

A helpful way to start singing your song is to imagine someone standing just behind the panel has made a challenging or confrontational remark. This can give you a sense of impetus for your first line. So, for example, suppose you were auditioning with the song, "I don't know how to love him" (see page 64). Imagine someone has just said, "What makes you think any man would want you?" Could this make the way you sing the opening line sound much more defiant and avoid sentimentality? Practise your audition song with friends who can come up with unexpected, thought-provoking questions.

Depending on time-constraints, the panel may let you sing the entire song or stop you halfway through. Try not to consider the latter to be a bad sign – they have probably heard everything they need and will often then want to hear a different vocal quality or a different dramatic intention to get a more rounded view of your potential.

The possibilities at this point are endless. The director may wish to work on a different interpretation of your song, or the musical director may wish to explore a specific musical point. Whatever the case, if you know your material well, you should be able to make a good attempt at whatever they ask.

At all times, keep positive and don't judge yourself. Often a panel/audience won't be aware of mistakes or changed lyrics unless you yourself draw attention to them. If you do forget a lyric, or a note doesn't quite come out how you intended, put it behind you at once and focus on the rest of the song. If, at the start of the song, you feel that the pianist hasn't grasped the tempo you want, don't be afraid to stop and reset the tempo rather than struggle through the whole song feeling uncomfortable. If you have taken your water bottle in with you, feel free to have a sip in between songs if you are feeling dry.

Very often a simple "Thank you, that will be all for today" from the panel will mark the end of your audition.

Exiting the room

Although this may sound a bit pedantic, don't forget that the panel will continue to form a picture of you as a person until the moment you step out of the room. Don't be afraid to ask questions about the project – remember that the audition is also a chance for you to find out if you get on with the creative team and are excited by the concept.

Once you have all finished, don't forget to collect your music and thank the pianist (who always gains a couple of new music books left by candidates during a full day of auditions). A simple thank you and goodbye will then normally suffice – particularly if faced with a panel of ten when handshakes would turn into an embarrassingly prolonged experience.

The waiting game

> *Real talent isn't always immediately classifiable. It can't be defined by whether or not you get a job.*
>
> Matt Ryan (director)

In the hours and days after an audition, it can be quite easy to wind yourself up – particularly if you don't hear anything. Try not to judge yourself – it is very difficult to analyse your own performance and often it is after auditions where you think you've done badly that you receive a recall. If you have an agent, they will ring you as soon as they know anything. It is not a good idea to keep telephoning or emailing the production company or casting director directly – they simply don't have time to handle such queries. You should presume that if you've heard nothing after a couple of weeks, it really is a case of "not this time". Unfortunately, it is not usual to get much feedback from the early rounds of auditions for large musicals. But do remember that the casting director may well put a note about you on your CV and ask to see you for a subsequent show.

Putting a show together is like a jigsaw puzzle. This means that there is a mental picture of a show and the casting director will be working on it piece by piece. Each piece of the puzzle will be determined by those already in place.

David Grindrod (casting director)

The audition panel

It is a good idea to find out in advance who is on the audition panel. You may not be able to find out everything, but you will almost certainly be able to find out the name of the director, musical director and choreographer. At the very least, you should ask the stage-management when you get to your audition. If you aren't already familiar with their background, look on the web to see what they've done. It may give you an idea of the way they work and might be useful in conversation.

> *Always check out your director and musical director. Look at what they've done before and what they're likely to appreciate.*
>
> David Grindrod (casting director)

If you've ever wondered what the people behind the audition desk actually do on a production, here is a brief outline of their roles:

Stage-management

The first person you meet when you arrive will be one of the stage-management team. They will announce you as you enter the room and may introduce the panel to you. They will pass on CVs and photos if the panel doesn't already have copies. Stage-management is in charge of what happens in the stage area and will usually be very close to the casting director, so try to make a good impression.

Casting director

The casting director and their team will have organised the auditions. Having been introduced by the stage-manager, it is often the casting director who will want to chat to you first. They will have received your CV and photo and are employed by the producer to find an interesting mix of performers for the creative team to meet. They will have a breakdown of roles and will have decided which you might be suitable for. Your agent may have given you some idea of the part or parts you are being seen for, or you may just have been asked for "an up-tempo and a ballad". A recent trend has been for casting directors to hold a preliminary round of auditions with just themselves and a pianist – particularly if they are unfamiliar with an actor's work – before organising a session in front of the creative team.

It is worth remembering that, although you may not be what is wanted for that particular audition, you could well impress them with your ability and be put on file for subsequent jobs.

"THE CREATIVE TEAM"

Director

Even at an early stage of the production period, the director will have a strong vision for the show. Their job is to work with composers, writers, the rest of the creative team and the actors, to realise an overall vision for the project. Although they will almost certainly have a large – if not the final – say in the casting, at a preliminary stage everything is up for grabs. They will be looking for a performer who will not only help express the director's own ideas, but has a creative imagination of their own. The director may want to work on your prepared material with you to see if you can take direction and interpret their ideas. They may also work on spoken text with you.

Resident director

For longer-running/big-budget musicals, there may also be a resident director present at your audition. Their role is to keep the show up and running once the director has moved on, and to rehearse understudies/covers. Their input at auditions can be crucial and they will consider it important to have personalities that can work well together. If they don't know you, they may contact colleagues or teachers with whom you have worked for a reference.

Musical director

Sometimes the musical director will be playing for your audition, although they will still be concentrating carefully on your performance. They will be listening not only to your interpretation and vocal ability but also to see if your voice sounds healthy enough to sing eight shows a week. They will quite frequently ask you to do a few technical exercises to explore your range. They will usually stay with the show for its duration, except in the case of long-running West-End shows.

Musical supervisor

Big-budget shows now often have a musical supervisor whose job is to oversee all aspects of the show's musical life, from vocal arrangements to orchestration and casting. Both the supervisor and the musical director will be looking for singers who can fulfil the musical score and its vocal demands: of the entire panel, they often have the most specific demands.

Choreographer

Depending on the type of show, you may be asked to do a separate dance call with the choreographer. They will be looking out for people with a strong technique and who can pick up combinations easily. However, even in your singing audition, a choreographer will be looking at your body language and physicality as you deliver your song and move about the room.

Composer, book writer and lyricist

These are sometimes the same person, sometimes two, sometimes three. If they are involved in casting, they will certainly have opinions about what they are looking for, although these will have been discussed at length with the creative team.

Producer

A producer has to be concerned with finance. However, most often they are in this business because they genuinely love the theatre and have idealistic aims. Some will make sure that they are actively involved in the embryonic stages of a musical and will have invested much time and passion – as well as money – in it. They are often in the room during the audition period, particularly during the later stages of casting, and will have strong opinions which will be taken into account by the creative team.

Company manager

For some (particularly long-running) shows, a company manager will be present to look after the creative team during the audition process. Like the resident director, the company manager will be with the show long after the departure of the creative team so they will be interested in your attitude, punctuality, etc.

Pianist

Make the piano your friend and the pianist your brother.

Liza Minnelli

Read the above quotation then read it again and again. It might just prove to be one of the most important bits of advice in this book. Arguably, the pianist, over and above the director or producer, is the most important person to you during your audition. Not only will you be making music together for the next few minutes, the way you interact with your accompanist will speak volumes about how you will behave in the rehearsal room. The pianist will need a clear copy of your music, accurately and legibly marked up, and will expect you to take time to explain the tempo, style and the structure of the piece. No matter how nervous you may feel, or how keen you are to get your audition over and done with, do yourself a favour and take this time to make sure the pianist has a fighting chance of playing what you expect to hear. It will pay off and you won't feel quite so alone on the floor.

Theatre manners

How to present yourself

It can seem that people in the theatre are very "free and easy" – but there are unwritten rules and disciplines which, if adhered to, create an atmosphere which is conducive to true freedom of thought and expression.

- PUNCTUALITY AT ALL TIMES! Be where you're needed when you're needed.
- It's the performer's responsibility always to be ready.
- If you have to leave the audition space at any time (e.g. to visit the loo), make sure the stage-manager knows where you are.
- Generosity to performers around you: be aware of other people's needs. This is most often noticed in dance auditions where you are sharing the floor with other performers.
- Show that you are listening and responsive to ideas given by the panel.
- Never go to an audition if you aren't available for the job – unless the casting director has specifically asked you to (this is rare). If they are interested but you aren't available, you are wasting their time and could damage a future relationship.
- Switch off your mobile phone.

Don't go if you have no intention of going for the job – don't go just to be seen.

Jill Green (casting director)

Gate-crashing auditions

This means turning up unannounced at an audition with your CV and photos and trying to get past the stage-manager (who will have a list of timings for named people). On rare occasions, this may work, but usually it is just an annoyance. Decide if you are that desperate!

Where to look during your audition

This is a very common question – it can feel far more daunting singing to a panel of two people than to an audience of 2,000. Directors seem to have different preferences and your decision will depend on the nature of your material and the size of the room or theatre.

I love actors who sing directly to me in auditions. Mind you, be selective about this – it makes some people very uncomfortable. Don't coerce the panel or turn them into your acting partner. Just express your real feelings to them.

Matt Ryan (director)

If you are performing a song that has direct audience communication – particularly comic numbers – then it is great to engage the panel. They will generally be more comfortable being directly addressed with a character song than with a heart-wrenching ballad. It will also depend on the role you are auditioning for: if you were being seen for the Emcee in *Cabaret* or for any other narrator-type role, then you should certainly show that you are comfortable at communicating in a very direct way.

If you decide not to address the panel directly, where should you direct your focus? This can be difficult if you don't know the space. If it is a theatre, the best thing to do is put your focus at the back of the stalls. If you are in a room or a small hall, aim just beyond the panel.

Filming your audition

It has become quite commonplace for auditions to be filmed – particularly if the creative team or producer are abroad. You will usually be told either to ignore the camera or possibly to direct your thoughts straight to the camera. Listen carefully to what you are asked to do and ask if you are not sure.

You may not be told in advance about filming. Don't let it throw you.

Things you may be asked to try out with your prepared material

As I have already mentioned, you should aim to deliver a personal and distinctive performance of your prepared material. A director is looking for artists with a point of view. Equally, they are looking for actors who can take direction and take notes quickly.

> *There is a temptation to deliver what you think they (the panel) want. You need to concentrate on the song – you can't just sing the notes! Don't try to "please" – you have a view, but be prepared to change it if asked.*
>
> Trevor Jackson (casting director)

Here are some ideas that might be put to you:

Try it in your own/in a different dialect This can feel strange to a singer – different accents make different shapes in the mouth. Experiment beforehand, with reference to the musical you are auditioning for. Also, much repertoire comes from the US and hearing the song in your own accent can sometimes lead you to show a much more truthful performance, but it can feel bizarre if you haven't practised it.

Move about the room When you're nervous, you can easily become stiff and look too formal. If you're lucky enough to have a director or choreographer who recognises this, they may ask you to move freely around the room. They may even suggest you roll around on the floor as you sing. Practise it – it can free your voice and feel fantastic. N.B. Only do this if asked!

Use a prop you weren't expecting If your song has an obvious reference to a prop, object, or other person, the director may try to incorporate this into your performance. This can also be a method of getting you to forget about the formality of the audition situation and focus on a dramatic situation. At a final audition for *The Far Pavilions*, the director Gale Edwards asked one of the actresses to sing a lullaby to her rucksack, pretending it was her child. The actress did it with total conviction and got the job.

Try a different key This is fairly standard – it's not necessarily about how high or low you can sing but often more about exploring the different colours in your voice.

Speak the lyrics as a monologue When doing this, make sure you are not just copying the rhythm of the music. Practise doing this out loud as it can really throw you at an audition.

The audition process

First round

This doesn't take long – it's an occasion when "Thank you – that's all we need for today" rings true. The panel will quickly decide whether you might be right for their project. Remember that this stage may take a number of weeks for big shows, so don't expect to hear straight away – if at all!

Second round

This is where you may hear the phrase, "in the mix". This means the team are clarifying their ideas and trying to begin the job of putting the right people together. You may be sent music to learn – often at the last minute. Try to memorise it, no matter how little time you are given – it will give you a better chance to show yourself well.

Further recalls

This is where it can get nerve-racking, as you know you are being seriously considered for a job!

If you are being considered for a principal role or cover, you may be asked to sing with somebody else. The panel will expect you to be able to work well with another artist – generosity to a fellow performer is always appreciated.

For ensembles, directors will often hold a workshop in which they bring together the actors they are interested in. This will often take the form of a warm-up and improvisation games, followed by work on material from the show. Again, this will indicate your ability to work with other people and take direction.

It is worth remembering that at this stage, for the long-running shows, it is not always clear who is leaving the cast. You can do nothing about this so keep an open mind!

Dance auditions

The casting director will usually tell you the style of dance in advance – e.g. in the style of Bob Fosse, Arlene Phillips, Susan Stroman. It is worth finding out as much as you can about the choreographer's work – the internet has made life easy in this respect. As a general note, keep yourself aware of different styles by seeing examples of different choreographers' work.

Procedure on the day

As with any audition, make sure you get there nice and early to get changed and to warm up. When you arrive, you will often be asked to fill out a card with your details and you will then be assigned to a large group (usually of about 20). If you have to wait around, it can be hard to keep your focus – be patient! Once you get in the room, most dance captains will give you time to warm up but you should have a quick stretch outside beforehand – just in case. You will learn your combination all together as a group and will then usually be broken into groups of around five in order for the creative team to take a look at you.

> *I look for people who are ready to 'go for it'. They want to be in the room.*
>
> Jill Green (casting director)

The way you conduct yourself in the audition will tell just as much about personality, training and ability as your dancing. Having chatted with some top choreographers, here are some thoughts to bear in mind:

- Don't be disheartened if you are put next to someone who triple-pirouettes their way through the audition – it isn't always the best dancers who are chosen. The panel may like you for something you haven't thought of. Always give 100% effort.

- Inexperienced auditionees judge what they think the panel wants by looking at types already in the group. It could be coincidental that they are all tall or short – don't prejudge body types. Two musicals that choose less conventional body types are *Billy Elliot* and *Acorn Antiques*. For these shows, people's shapes and sizes are irrelevant but they have to be prepared to dance.

- When you are given a position on the floor, hold it. Being at the back doesn't matter: the given formation means that you can still be seen – it's been organised for the benefit of all. Be spatially aware and generous to other dancers.

- If you are unclear, ask to see the combination again. If the choreographer asks, "Everybody all right?", don't be frightened to ask to see it again, if you need to – as long as your questions are relevant. However, don't ask in order to be noticed – just be genuine.

- When learning a combination, don't think you are being judged – concentrate on what the choreographer is teaching you. You don't need to "perform" yet – just get the combination right. Choreographers are looking to see if people are able to concentrate, even when marking.

- Reserve a bit of energy so that by the time you get to a small group – if you're given the chance – you haven't burned yourself out. And don't disappear and go home after your turn – you may be asked to do it again.

- If you aren't up to it and the audition feels beyond you, it's better to say so to the panel. It is not held against you in the future.

- For musical theatre in particular, your job is to tell a story through dance.

The dance routine is usually part of the story and, although technique is valued by the choreographer, it alone doesn't communicate character – which is really important.

Stephen Mear (choreographer)

Clothes for dance auditions

Whatever your standard, make sure you are well-equipped for your dance audition. Take a bag which contains:

Girls:

1) jazz shoes (split-sole Capezio shoes are good all-rounders)
2) tap shoes
3) heels
4) ballet shoes

Boys:

1) jazz shoes
2) tap shoes

3) ballet shoes

You will also need a change of clothes and spare T-shirts.

Here are some clothing thoughts:

- Tracksuits don't show off your legs. For jazz auditions, wear stretch trousers.

- Show individuality by wearing something memorable. For example, green shoes, pink hair-piece, a bandana – anything that makes a casting director look towards you.

- Show your shape. Beware of the tied jumper round your waist.

- Before going to your audition, check carefully what the advert says (e.g. "full make-up and heels", "fishnets").

- No baseball cap – you'll be asked to take it off.

- Make sure your hair doesn't hide your face (tie back that fringe).

Actors'/singers' movement

Even if you don't consider yourself to be a dancer as such, you will still be called on to demonstrate what is generally called "movement". In an audition, candidates will be given a simple routine to show character. Choreographers look for you to be "comfortable on stage" – i.e. walk, sit and stand entirely naturally and be able to pick up a combination of steps of varying difficulty. Much of this part of the audition process is to do with showing that you are willing to be brave and have a go.

You can tell when they love "having a go" to the best of their ability and – most important – are enjoying it. In which case, I would be more prepared to take a chance on them. Some singers at auditions say "I don't dance" in a negative way – this is no good for me. I look for people willing to have a really good go at the combination.

Stephen Mear (choreographer)

Look out for training opportunities and classes. Even if you are not a dancer, they will help you gain confidence. They should cover at least some of the following:

- Actors warm-up: not a dance class but prepares students for the class.
- Movement relating to freeing the voice.
- Neutral posture – freedom from unnecessary tension.
- Physical co-ordination.
- Characterisation and improvisation.
- An exploration of the use of space.

Maintaining yourself between auditions

I've talked in this book about the audition day itself, but what about the days, weeks and maybe even months between auditions? Vocal and physical health go together – they are completely connected. It is important to keep physically healthy to maintain vocal health.

Keep in shape mentally. Stimulate your mind – visit the theatre, cinema and exhibitions regularly. Read as many libretti and plays as you can and familiarise yourself with a diverse range of musical theatre – not just the shows currently in the West End or on tour.

If you find the period between auditions stressful, try to engage in relaxing activities which help you to stay focused. Meditation is a great way to still your mind, but needs practice. There are many methods available – you can usually find details of what's on offer at a local health-food shop or health centre.

Your career is for a lifetime. If you don't get a particular job, try to see it in context – you would have liked it but don't actually need it. This should help you relax and keep positive.

Keeping the vocal folds and throat well-lubricated is really important. The best thing is to drink pure water. Make this a regular habit and keep a water bottle near you so you are always well-hydrated. But don't get obsessed by this – about two litres of water a day is ample. Also, many fruits and vegetables have high water content.

Eat well and keep physically fit. Dance practice helps keep you fit – go to regular classes. Circuit training or aerobic exercise is good for the cardio-vascular system – it gets your heart pumping and is good for your breathing.

Weight-training makes you look and feel good. However, make sure you learn correct breathing for this – wrongly done it can put unnecessary tension on your laryngeal muscles and vocal folds and can cause damage. It can also make you muscle-bound, so be sure to maintain physical flexibility.

The following forms of exercise are widely practised and are often available quite cheaply at a local leisure centre:

- Gym
- Swimming
- Alexander technique
- Feldenkreis
- Pilates

Ongoing training

> *Whether you have done a full-time training course or not, it is important to continue developing your skills throughout your career.*
>
> Trevor Jackson (casting director)

Ongoing training, be it a weekly dance class or the occasional session with a good singing teacher or coach, will make all the difference, not only in keeping your skills sharp but also in keeping a positive mental attitude in between jobs and auditions.

Classes to support your training are available. Details of some of these can be found from the following websites:

- www.actorscentre.co.uk
- www.pineapple.uk.com
- www.danceworks.co.uk
- www.actorstemple.com
- www.youngblood.co.uk

Alternatively, search online for classes in your area.

Singing lessons

Finding the right teacher for *you* is essential. Recommendations from friends and colleagues are usually the best. As a singing teacher and vocal coach myself, I would say don't feel disloyal if you want to try someone else. All teachers have specialist areas and different ways of working, and different people respond to different ideas.

A singing teacher should first and foremost be a good technical teacher. Some also have the ability to coach – which means working on the interpretation of songs. This is good financially – particularly if you are preparing for an audition – as you get "two for the price of one" . It can be hard to find someone who is familiar with contemporary voice techniques, although more and more teachers are attending seminars and learning about this. If you're not sure where to start looking, you could check which teachers are members of the British Voice Association or the Association of Teachers of Singing.

Repertoire coach

A coach should have a good knowledge of many styles of musical-theatre repertoire. They should be able to advise you about suitable songs for you and to put them on a tape or CD for you to rehearse to. Make sure they put new tunes down very slowly to give you time to listen carefully. It is also important to practise with a recording of the printed accompaniment (which may not include the tune) so you have no surprises at the audition.

Repertoire coaches are often found by word of mouth – ask for recommendations on musical-theatre courses or other places of study (check out the noticeboards at places like The Actors' Centre or music colleges).

Fringe shows, profit-share and paid work in amateur companies

These are opportunities to perform and keep your brain active. It's not so easy to get this kind of work now because so many people want to do it. The problem is being able to afford to pay your bills, as most of this work is poorly paid (if at all) but nevertheless well worth doing. You can find out about these opportunities through reading *The Stage*, for example, but mostly it will be through the personal contacts you make. Sometimes your agent may be asked to recommend artists for fringe shows.

Jobs between auditions

It is a fact of life that it's unusual to go straight from one theatre job to the next. Most of us need to earn money to live. A helpful word of advice is to remember that many jobs can be hard on the voice. If you are teaching Saturday-morning classes, working in call centres, demonstrating toys at Christmas, doing cosmetic promotions – the list is endless – keep hydrated and be aware that the way you use your speaking voice affects your singing. You can't repair a tired voice in a couple of hours. Try to have a habitually healthy voice: you're not being over-cautious – it's one of the tools of your trade. Always apply your training to everyday life (see the section *Speaking voice* on page 99).

Workshops

If you get a chance to participate in a workshop with a professional director or MD, it is a good idea to try out your audition material. This will give you another perspective and see how you cope with performing under different circumstances and in other environments. These events are often advertised in the industry magazines and on the noticeboards of many training centres.

New musicals

If you have an opportunity to take part in the development of new material, paid or unpaid, **grab it!** It can be inspiring creatively and you never know – it might get taken up and you could be part of that process. For example, *Jerry Springer: The Opera* was developed at Battersea Arts Centre and at the Edinburgh Festival and went on to the National Theatre, West End and on tour.

USEFUL INFORMATION

Spotlight *and other casting publications*

Spotlight
7 Leicester Place
London
WC2H 7RJ
02074377631

This is a photographic dictionary used by everyone in the business.

Spotlight publication deadlines:

Actors (published annually in April):

- New photo entry deadline: 14th October
- Same photo entry deadline: 1st November
- Interim entries: from February onwards

Actresses (published annually in October):

- New photo entry deadline: 15th April
- Same photo entry deadline: 1st May
- Interim entries: from August onwards

Children (published annually in May):

- Deadline for all entries: 15th November
- Interim entries: from April onwards

Graduates (published annually in February):

- 2/3-year course entries deadline: 15th October

- Postgraduate course entries: 24th November

Presenters (published annually in January):

- Deadline for all entries: 10th July
- Interim entries: from October onwards

It is essential to be in *Spotlight*. Try to manage a half-page photo and think carefully about which section you should be in.

Spotlight is available via the internet (popular with agents and casting directors) and in book form. It currently costs £124 to subscribe annually.

Contacts

Contacts is the Yellow Pages for actors. This doesn't contain casting information but is published annually by *Spotlight* and has addresses and phone numbers of theatres, agents, casting directors and lots of information.

- Published annually in November
- Deadline for submitting freeline entries: end of June
- Deadline for advertising: mid-July

The Stage

A weekly newspaper which contains ads, but it is also useful to read what shows are being put on and who is directing them, both in London and elsewhere.

PCR (Production and Casting Report)

A weekly production and casting report which includes ads for commercial productions and films. Available over the internet to subscribers (a printed copy is also sent out).

Websites for work

These function in one of three ways:

Advert/newsgroup postings You usually pay a small activation fee or a monthly or yearly contribution to access the noticeboards. Then you can search the jobs posted and apply for them either directly, using the email or address details provided, or through the website. Examples of these are:

- www.mandy.com
- www.starnow.com

Many of these websites also have an email service – they send you details of the latest postings daily or weekly with a link to the website.

Personal web pages These function like a searchable database online, much like the *Spotlight* pages. They vary as to how much detail they allow you to include on your web page, and some also enable you to upload sound clips as well as digital images. You are entirely responsible for the content of your own web page, therefore it is prudent to exercise caution when uploading personal information. Never use a website asking you to publicise any banking details, and only put address information up if you are happy to receive mail (even visits) from total strangers. These websites vary in price from free to several hundred pounds per year. Here are a couple of the more reputable ones:

- www.actorsingerdancer.co.uk
- www.castingcallpro.com

Generally, I'd say the best way to judge these sites is to check out who already uses them – if there is no one you have ever heard of and there is a hefty fee, don't bother.

At the time of writing, www.myspace.com is one of the best ways to promote yourself – it is a great way to post information about and photos of yourself, and it's free.

Online agencies Some of these are casting agencies, some of them call themselves personal managers. Most of them handle models as well as actors, singers and dancers. They generally charge a fee plus commission if you get work through them. They function in much the same way as the personal web pages hosted by other sites. Some examples of these are:

- www.talentnetworks.com
- www.castingfiles.com

The best way to find work online, however, is to do a search with the relevant key-words. These should include words that describe yourself (e.g. singer, twenties, female, paid, film, casting) and the area you live in or are prepared to travel to for work (e.g. London, south-east).

INTERVIEWS

TRACIE BENNETT

Tracie Bennett trained at the Italia Conti Academy in London. She appeared in the TV soap Coronation Street *between 1982 and 1984 and again in 1999, and played Malandra in the film* Shirley Valentine. *She has twice won Olivier awards for Best Performance in a Supporting Role in a Musical, for her performances in* She Loves Me *and* Hairspray.

I'll never forget my very worst audition – it was for *Follies* in the West End, with Mike Ockrent directing. I'd got through all the preliminary auditions – where you turn up and they ask you if you can dance and sing, so you do a few steps and sing a few bars and then they say "Next"! Well, I'd got through the first four of those and now I was on audition number five and I was due to meet Mike Ockrent.

This was an acting audition and that is the one that I generally have to do the least work for. After all, I am an actor – or so I thought. So, I'm on this West-End stage and I'm listening to him and thinking about what he's asking me to do, but I'm just not getting it. There are twenty people out there in the darkened auditorium, all here to watch me do my stuff and, although this is supposed to be the easy bit, I'm just not doing it right.

So finally he has to get up on the stage and explain it to me. He's brilliant Mike Ockrent, but I'm looking at him and I'm just not getting it – I don't know why. I think the adrenaline kicks in, and you're almost bolting off the starting line, without waiting for the starting gun. It wasn't nerves in the normal sense of the word, it was just that I wanted to do really well. But that's something you have to control.

Having got through the first four auditions, you'd think that it should get easier. But it doesn't. The pressure gets much greater, because now they are really looking at you. And I'm getting embarrassed – I'm thinking I should know what you're talking about. So I tell myself to stop and breathe and listen.

I've thought back about that over the years and I'd now know not to take things so personally. I have stopped thinking about me. I've discovered – and this is my own way of working – that I can't be Tracie Bennett in that room. I have to blank me out and then blank out the room. After that, I try and mould myself to what it is they are looking for. I have to really listen to direction. You have to stop thinking about them out there watching what you are doing. You have to stop wondering how you are getting on. Get rid of self-awareness – it stops creativity. You cannot have fear.

So with Mike Ockrent, there I am doing my very best to give him what he wants – and I'm through! Audition Number Six. Every American member of the team has come over. Mike Ockrent's there again, plus Sondheim, who's like a god for me, and the MD – it felt like millions of them.

I arranged to bring my own pianist, Simon Lee, who is brilliant. Some of that music is really difficult, but Simon could do it in his sleep and having him there meant that I had someone on my side. It's winter outside and it's snowing. I have on this huge Russian greatcoat that touches the ground. After the audition, I'm catching a train back to Manchester, so I have this huge suitcase with me. And a holdall, which has my life in it. Everything that's important to me is in this holdall. My music, my money, all the Christmas presents I've wrapped, my passport. Everything.

Because I'm bagged down, I decide to go into town for the audition even earlier than usual and, with so much time to kill, I go to a café for a carrot juice to calm me down. It's got a really peaceful atmosphere – full of nuns and gentle people, potters and teachers all having their vegetarian fare. My bags are really heavy so I leave them at a table near the door. I'm waiting in the queue and I see this man come in. The first thing that occurs to me is that he's a bit of a weirdo. Just the way he starts looking around the place, I know there's something not quite right about him. He's looking shifty. And he's wearing this huge coat. As he's standing near my cases, I see him sort of shrug off his coat – he shrugs it off and it's lying on the top of my holdall. Then he sort of gathers it back up again and I see what he's doing. I realise he's going to steal my bag and I think: "No you don't. I've got my life in there. My contact lenses! Everything to do with *Follies*, all my notes!"

So, there's me in my Russian greatcoat – I become like Batman swooping across the restaurant. And he's out the door with my holdall and I'm up the street after him. He's bigger than me, but I don't care. There are things in that holdall that I can't replace and he's not having them. I jump at him and I've got my arm locked round his neck and he's lashed out at me and hit me in the mouth, but I don't know that yet. And we're both on the ground in the snow and there's blood all over the place, but I don't know that yet either. All those nuns and potters are watching through the window and no one comes out to help me. He's hitting at my face and I'm pulling at him and somehow he slips out of his coat and runs off. But I still have my holdall.

Next thing, the manager of the café comes out – now that the man has gone. When he helps me up, I see the blood all over the snow. It looks like pints and pints of it. I walk back into the restaurant to get my suitcase. I'm single-minded. This man was an interruption. I have an audition to go to.

The manager wants me to stay: he's called the police. "They'll be here in a second," he says. I don't care. "I'll call them later," I say. I've worked for weeks and weeks for this audition. Sondheim is here. I'm not going to be late.

I still haven't seen my face. Later I discover that I've got a split lip, my earring has been half torn off, I've cuts and scratch marks down my cheeks and there's blood everywhere. But right now I feel no pain. The adrenaline is rushing through me and there is only one thing I care about.

The manager makes me stay and everyone is staring at me. But sure enough, two coppers show up in less than a minute. "I'm not giving a statement," I tell them, "I've got an audition to go to." I look back on this now and think, what was I like? They wanted to call an ambulance and I said no. It was my choice, wasn't it? They couldn't keep me, I'd done nothing wrong. That audition was so important to me; more important than anything. And I'd worked really hard for it.

So, these coppers really get into it and decided they'd come with me! They came with me to the theatre – I have a police escort! They even carried my bags.

We get into the theatre and the stage-door keeper just looks at my face and I have to ask him if I can use the toilet. I go downstairs and that's when I see myself for the first time. I'm a mess. My lip is really swollen, my eyes are starting to shut, I'm cut all over the place. I wash myself with cold water and I slap on some make-up to cover up the worst of it and I start to try and get myself together.

The police come with me to the wings. They think it's all great! Really exciting! And they wish me luck. Simon's there already. We haven't had a chance to speak. He doesn't know what has happened. So there I am on the stage. Out front is Stephen Sondheim with all the American team.

I start to sing. But by now everything has swollen up and I can hardly open my jaw. I start to sing and the sound that comes out is terrible. I'm caterwauling. I'm like a tom-cat on a garden fence in the middle of the night. Simon is staring at me. The casting director is staring at me with a look of horror on her face. The policemen are watching from the wings. I sing the song. I get through it. And you know what Sondheim said at the end? "Great piano playing." That was it. I knew I hadn't got it. I went back with the police and gave my statement. Then I got the train back up north, went home and cried for two days.

Maybe I should have told them what had just happened. But you see, I've been brought up with the notion that you leave yourself outside the door when you go for an audition. They weren't there to hear about me – they were there to see what I could do. And besides, this was the only day they were available. They weren't going to fly the American team back over, at a cost of $5,000, just to see me. That was my chance and, for whatever reason, I blew it. Not that I would have got it anyway – Gillian Bevan played the role and she was brilliant, far better than I would have been. But still, that was definitely my worst audition.

I've been acting for more than thirty years now and one of the reasons that I think I'm still lucky enough to get work is that I don't mind changing with the job. You know the way, when you are seven, you see this beautiful pair of dream shoes in a shop window and you really, really want them. So you wish for them and wish for them and finally you get them for your birthday. And you love them completely but two months later they are too small for you.

Well, I move on to the next pair of shoes and the next. I've played young things. And then you start getting mother-of-a-young-baby parts, and so it goes on. Now that my face is starting to slip, I'm good at ageing prostitutes and drug addicts. And I don't knock it. There are some great parts out there. Why try and stay the same young thing when there are younger things coming up behind you all the time? Be realistic. I'm brave enough to try new things – even at the risk of being no good – in order to learn. I look forward to each new phase.

The other reason that I think I'm still lucky enough to get work is to do with sowing seeds. I've done it all my life. You can't afford to be a snob. Go anywhere, if you dare, to learn new skills. Have faith in others casting you in parts you might not think you are right for – stretch your comfort zone.

I'm aware when I go to an audition that I am an ambassador for the person who has recommended me, be it the casting director or my agent, or even for the project I'm going for. That's why I was cast as the voice of Bridget Jones in the talking book version. The woman from the publishing house had seen me on a chat show talking about a sitcom I was in. She decided that I was Bridget Jones and tracked me down. And I'm saying: "Have you got the right girl? Are you sure?" That's what I mean about the importance of being a good ambassador. It's about always being professional.

There's a sequel to the *Follies* story. Cut to maybe ten years later and an audition for *She Loves Me*. They called me in and were so nice, I couldn't believe it. This was the American team who'd done the show on Broadway and won a Tony award. And I'm thinking, why are they being so nice to me? The audition went really well and I got offered the part there and then. It turns out they'd talked to Mike Ockrent in New York and he said, there's only one girl in London who should play that part and that was me. Even when I was at my worst, he'd remembered me.

They'd called me in just to check me out really. So it turns out that the worst audition in the world, in a funny sort of a way, actually led me to getting the job that won me an Olivier award. Of course, I didn't think like that at the time. So always go to an audition, no matter what – you never know where it might lead.

PHILIP QUAST

Philip Quast trained in Australia at NIDA (National Institute of Dramatic Arts). He played Javert in Les Misérables *both in Australia and in the West End. In 1991 he was awarded the first of three Olivier awards for his performance as George in* Sunday in the Park with George *at the National Theatre. Other credits include roles in* The Fix, South Pacific, The Secret Garden, Evita *and* La Cage aux Folles.

Because I work across the whole range of the media, I do many types of auditions. So it's hard to find one thing that is applicable to film, television or theatre. When I look at the auditions I've had to do, I have to say that I don't think I was very good at it – especially musical-theatre auditions. That's because I was always nervous. I always kept claiming that I wasn't a singer. Although I happen to have been blessed, or cursed in a way, with a good voice, people assumed I was musical. But I can't read music.

I always treated my auditions as part of the rehearsal process. I always felt, with a sort of arrogance, that the people auditioning me were using up my time and therefore treated it like, "I've got the part, now let me rehearse."

In auditions, I hope to show some kind of progression, show the panel that I could do something, sort of grab hold of it and show them that this was some kind of work in progress. So I'd do something for them and before they could say, "Thank you very much that's enough…" I'd jump in and say, "Right! I'd like to try it another way." And that was fine and worked a lot of the time, even though I'm sure that to some people it appeared arrogant. I felt, however, that it was the only way I could show how I could improve.

At the beginning, I was always nervous, but as I relaxed in the audition, I tried to make it into my time. The most pleasurable audition for me is one where we are all trying to invent something new in the room and where I can attempt to build up a relationship with the director and see if I can work with him or her. If, at the end of that time, I could feel that we had actually worked well together, that for me would be really exciting.

Of course, sometimes it wouldn't work out and in those instances it was just as well. I've always been quite philosophical about auditions. If I don't get the part, then it wasn't meant to be. If someone else got it, then they were meant to have it. You always need to be positive and look forward to the next audition. If you're bitter, it's negative and it's also destructive. I mean, realistically, you're not going to get every job.

I can bring my own experience to this. I teach now and also direct. Very often someone gets up and they are not great when they do their first song. Sometimes there might be just a little snippet that suggests they might have something special. You take that and you work with it. You see, all the best work I've done has emerged from auditions where I have been able to establish a collaborative relationship.

There's this theory that auditioning is good for you and that you should go and do it, whether or not you are right for the part. I disagree with this – I think it's damaging. You are sometimes putting yourself in a very painful place and bad memories from a bad audition can go on and infect a good audition later on.

I suppose it depends on who is there. If you are auditioning for one of the top directors – Sam Mendes, Michael Grandage, Trevor Nunn, Richard Eyre – I would go in just to be in the same rehearsal room with them. Rehearsal – that word is important because that's how these good directors treat the audition and you. They know what to do.

My best audition experience was also my worst. It was an audition for *Les Misérables*. I hadn't sung for two years and it was a cattle call of an audition! I was an established actor at the time, more an actor who could sing than a musical-theatre person.

I bounced into this big, long rehearsal room with huge windows behind me. Trevor wasn't there, but there were at least twenty people: directors, assistant directors, assistant producers and Cameron Mackintosh – all of them sitting behind desks. No one introduced themselves, and I didn't even know who Cameron Mackintosh was.

We'd been told to learn "Do you hear the people sing?" I'd sort of done that, but it goes very, very high. So I went up to the pianist, who I vaguely knew and said, "I don't know if I can sing this, it's so high!" And he said, "Don't worry. Everyone is having trouble." I had my other song, "Lucky Ol' Sun", on top of the piano as my fall back.

I think what bothered me right from the start was that I didn't feel as if I could take control of the audition in any way. It was just: In! Bang! Get on with it! So I started. I could vaguely hear feet move and wriggle and I began to hope that maybe some of them were thinking that I had an interesting voice. Then I got to the high bit and my voice cracked. I stopped. I cleared my throat and tried to make a joke of it. I said, "God, this is embarrassing! I'll start again." This was my way of attempting to take control of this situation and to turn it into a rehearsal. But the second time around the same thing happened. I was so completely embarrassed. Once again, I tried to laugh and make a joke of it. But no one else laughed.

And then a strange mixture of anger and embarrassment came over me because I was being subjected to this and no one in that room took it upon themselves to throw me a lifebuoy and say, "It's OK!" You see, there was no one director in charge because Trevor wasn't there. That was why I hadn't been able to work out to whom I should do the audition, or indeed who was looking after me. I started for the third time and pretty soon I realized it was going to happen again so I viciously grabbed my music off the piano and stormed out – audibly muttering profanities.

Cameron says now that at the time he was laughing. He thought it was hysterical. Anyway, he says that I'd turned on them all so viciously that they all thought at one and the same time "That's Javert!"

I wish I could claim credit for this as some kind of strategy, but that wasn't my intention. But it turned out it was the right thing to do. They came out and got me back and got me to sing some other stuff And I was through to the second auditions.

Now this audition was with Trevor Nunn and was a totally different experience. Of course it was. Trevor took control. It's the level of care he has. I sang the song and he came up to me and spoke about the character and the story. Then he asked me to sing it again to see how I'd interpreted the information he'd given me. In other words, we were rehearsing!

Then Trevor said, "You look a bit young. I mean, Javert is supposed to be…" And he took his coat off and draped it over my shoulders and stood back and then got me to sing it again. And at the end he came up to me and said, "I will see you in London." That was it! I was offered the part there and then. So my worst audition had turned into an offer for *Les Misérables*.

From then on I started trying to treat all my auditions like rehearsals. I feel secure in this sort of process. And when you are secure you do the best that you can do. Your antennae go up. You listen. You relax vocally. You don't care if you make a bum sound because that, too, is part of the process.

SALLY ANN TRIPLETT

> *Sally Ann Triplett trained at the Arts Educational School. She has appeared in the West-End productions of* Follies, Chess, Grease, Cats, Anything Goes, Acorn Antiques, Chicago, Guys and Dolls *and* Take Flight. *Plays include Lady Beatrice in* Much Ado About Nothing *and Marge in* Absent Friends. *TV appearances include* Doctors, Down to Earth, Holby, EastEnders *and* The Bill.

A few years back, I was going for quite a lot of jobs at the same time. They were all really nice jobs apart from one that I wasn't too sure about. On the morning of the audition for the one that I wasn't sure about, I found out that I hadn't got one of the jobs I really wanted, even though I'd got right down to the final few. I was really quite upset about it and thought, when is it going to be my turn? I always seemed to be just behind the girl in front – I'm the one with lots of talent and really hard-working but never seem to get the luck.

Feeling like this, I went up for the other audition. Now, I've never ever done this before and I've never done it since, but on that day I just didn't care – I didn't care about it at all. I wasn't particularly upset about being turned down for that one job: it was a culmination of all the jobs I hadn't got. I was thinking: "When is it my turn?" I'm old enough. I've done enough work to prove myself, but I never seem to get the kind of jobs that everyone wants. I get nice stuff, but not the really nice stuff.

So I went in not caring. Now it turned out to be a rubbish job. But it doesn't matter what job it is or what you feel about it, you have to do your best. Otherwise, not only do you let down the people you're auditioning for, but you let yourself down. I was nearly asleep in the waiting room before I went in. I hadn't looked at my songs, I didn't even know what I was going to sing. I had three songs in my hand but I hadn't thought about them. And the woman asked me what I was going to sing and I chose one. I sang it like I was asleep. Afterwards she said: "OK, we're going to give you some music to learn. You come back and sing for us when you want to do it." She could tell straight away that I just couldn't be bothered.

I felt dreadful afterwards. I thought, that's disgusting. I can't do that again – I must always give every single audition the benefit of the doubt. No matter what has happened, you've got to turn it on. It's like doing a performance. Not that you have to be someone else – you have to be yourself, which can be difficult when you just don't feel up to it. But when you are doing a show or a play, night after night, you develop all these little anchors that you can hold on to get yourself through it. Last night, I didn't feel like performing at all – I felt tired and depressed, for no particular reason. I just didn't want to get out there and make people smile – I wanted to stay at home and watch the telly with my children. But you get out there and use these anchors to get you through and once you get going, it's all right.

When you've got an audition, it's your one chance: you have to be on top of it. You can spend weeks thinking about one particular audition, even just thinking about what you are going to wear.

One of the best auditions I've ever done was for *Anything Goes*. My dad was literally on his deathbed and I felt as if I had nothing to lose. It was only a week and a half before rehearsals began and they didn't know who they wanted. They had all these big names that were supposed to be doing it. It was the job of the year.

On the Friday my agent phoned and he said: "Look, it's been hard work but I've got you an audition, even though they didn't want to see you." I thought that was brilliant. I'd get to meet Trevor Nunn again. I'd get to see Stephen Mear, a friend of mine who was choreographing it. I'd get to go to the National Theatre and sing my songs. I wore a white suit – given my state of mind and everything that was going on, I looked fantastic.

I'd learned the songs off by heart. Sometimes I don't do that: I want to know them enough to show that I've worked on them, but that there's still a way to go. But this time I thought: "No, I just want to sing it. I'm going to try and be that person."

I was up for *Doctors* at the same time and it was only my second television part so I really wanted to get it. But part of me was still waiting to hear about this job at the National. It was a Thursday night and the rehearsals were due to start a week on Monday. I was in the playground with my daughter Grace and I took my mobile out of my pocket and looked at it. It said five forty and I knew my agent left at five thirty. But as I was holding it, it started to ring and it was him – my agent Barry. It was so weird. And he was more excited than I could possibly have been. He was completely over the moon. He couldn't contain himself at all. I'd got the job!

I think that is one of the best auditions I've ever done. And what did I learn from it? Well, you don't want a close member of your family dying. But somehow that affected me so much that it stripped other things away. I learned to be me. Also, the audition was for Trevor Nunn and he's a one-off. A lot of the time you are auditioning for people who don't know what they are looking for. Someone who has instinctive feelings about people is great to audition for because they can just say, "No, you're not right." And in that situation you always think, "Fine – at least they've told me straight away." But nowadays, six auditions is normal. You go, but think "What can I give them *this* time?"

This leads me on to *Chicago*. I'd auditioned in the very beginning along with Ruthie and Ute Lemper. But in my head, I wasn't fiery enough. I wasn't thinking: "I can do this." But after it had been running a year and I'd seen it on Broadway, I thought, "This is me – this is something I should be doing!" So when the audition came to take over, I went up for it. "Yeah, we liked that," they said. Next audition: "Yeah, yeah, we liked that." And I thought, "Well, I've done everything. Surely they know by now whether I'm the right person or not." So I asked my agent. "Am I up for Velma or for Roxy?" And he said: "I'm not sure. I think it might be either."

I thought, right, I'm going to wear a blonde wig. Everyone playing Velma so far has been a peroxide blonde. So maybe that's getting in their way. I got this fantastic peroxide wig, put on full slap, eyelashes, little black dress, everything.

I went in and they just couldn't believe it. I'd actually floored them with it. The idea of someone coming in with a blonde wig on – they couldn't get over the balls of it. I did the audition – all the Velma stuff. And at the end they said: "We want to see you do some Roxy stuff again." So I said, "Give me a minute," then went out and took the wig off and put my hair up really quickly and went back in – and they said, "Wow!"

As far as I was concerned, I'd got the job. I had the photographs taken. But at the eleventh hour, as Americans do – they're unpredictable – they gave it to someone else. Trevor Nunn would never think of doing that to anyone in a million years. I found that very, very hard to take. I hadn't signed a contract, so that was it.

I ended up doing another job as a fill in that I didn't want to do and I ended up staying in that job for a year and a half because it was brilliant money, but I was so depressed doing it.

As far as auditions go, I don't like to be spot-on with everything – I like to be a little more off-guard. I think it comes across as more natural. I'm more likely to sing along to the radio in the shower to warm myself up. I don't like to go over and over and over the song because then I just feel a bit robotic with it.

I don't have a huge portfolio of songs but I think I'm learning as I get older that you have to choose the right song for whatever you're going up for. If you don't have a suitable song, you have to learn a new one. And I need to learn it in advance so that I don't go in with the words swimming around in my head. I like to know it's in there and I can just bring it out.

So now, having done *Anything Goes*, I hope I won't have to prove myself as much again because everyone will have seen the show and know that I can do it. So I'm not going to be seventh on the list. Hopefully, I'll be second or third. Or maybe even first. You never know.

But you still have to go in there and do the audition. There's a job coming up next year. I know it's a comedy and I'm already wondering what I am going to sing.

CLIVE ROWE

Clive Rowe trained at the Guildhall School of Music and Drama. His musical-theatre credits include Nicely-Nicely Johnson in the National Theatre's revival of Guys 'n' Dolls *(for which he won an Olivier award), Mr Snow in* Carousel, *Dink in* Carmen Jones *and Mr Cellophane in* Chicago. *He has performed Pompey in* Measure for Measure *at the Royal Shakespeare Company and Thersites in* Troilus and Cressida *at Regent's Park Theatre.*

I have lots of memories of good auditions but not really any bad ones. When I left the Guildhall School of Music and Drama, I'd already done my first professional job, which was *Carmen Jones* in Sheffield. I think I had a kind of naivety that got me through my early auditions without too much stress. I was nervous about doing an audition but didn't have that feeling that I've developed as I've got older – that need to please. I think we all have that as actors. You feel you've got to please the director and the MD. You find you can't concentrate on what you're doing, you have to concentrate on who is there and how they are listening.

I know there are people who go into auditions and are really blasé about it – it's just about the job. But I know for myself – and this may be a failing of mine – I have a real need to please people. When I go into an audition, I need to be liked by the people, whether they want me for the job or not.

In many ways, if you can lessen that need to please you can feel more confident when you go into the room. And knowing that you are right for what you are going for is a really, really big thing. I've been in the business for nearly twenty years, so I have confidence in my abilities and, as I've got older, my audition perspective has narrowed. But it's not something you have experience of when you are starting out.

My very first audition was for Trevor Nunn. It was for *Porgy and Bess* at Glyndebourne. The only other audition I'd done before that was to get into drama school. I remember going into the audition and naivety being a big shield. I had no real concept of what I was auditioning for. I knew I was auditioning for *Porgy and Bess*, but I had no concept of Trevor Nunn, one of the world's greatest directors of musicals, or of Glyndebourne, one of the great operatic stages in Britain, if not the world. I just thought I was going up for a part in a musical.

This meant that many of my early auditions were, while not easy, calm. I'd never go in thinking, "Oh no, it's the National Theatre and it's *Guys and Dolls* second time round." I'd only ever be thinking about the part.

Nerves, if anything, make me forget my lines and my knees start shaking – what I call cabaret knee. In the one or two auditions where this has happened, it was because I felt unprepared. Normally, this is when I have been given a song that I don't feel entirely comfortable with. I like to take a long time to learn my songs. The longer you have, the more settled you are with them.

In an audition, I always feel that, by the end of the first eight bars of a song, they know whether or not you can sing it, what your interpretation's like – more or less everything. So the first eight bars are the most important part of the song. But the first bar – that's my worst. I need time to settle myself with the material so I feel confident I can just open my mouth and sing it. You get to the point where you know it so well that you can make people believe it is fresh, where you seem to be searching for the next line all the time. It's probably quite exhilarating to watch someone who is not sure of their work, who has that edge, who is just grasping for each new thought and pulling it in. But, as a performer, you don't want to do that because it is a very dangerous place to be.

The perfect musical-theatre audition for me would be one where they would say, "Sing something that you know already." Or to have either two weeks or two days to prepare a song. Not anything in between. If you have four or five days, you have enough time to get worried about it but not enough time to work on it properly. If you have two days, then you learn it, you get up, you warm up, you go and do the audition. There's nothing more you can do about it. With two weeks you can start working on it properly. I spend, if I'm being honest, maybe twenty minutes a day. Then as the audition gets closer, forty or forty-five minutes just on that particular song. But some days I don't do anything at all, because I don't want to get uptight about it.

What you want to avoid is that third voice – the little voice outside that goes "Oh! Oh dear!" It might start when you go out of the audition but it doesn't matter then. You just don't need that voice in your ear when you are in the middle of an audition. There are enough people watching you already without having you watch yourself. It's about getting yourself to a level where it should almost be automatic when you walk through that door. I don't mean that everything you are doing in that room is a performance. You want to be relaxed. Emotionally, you want to engage with the people there.

My good experiences have also come out of the fact that I've auditioned for really good people. Really good directors make you feel comfortable as soon as you walk into their space. That's really important. A great director understands the stress you're under before you even get in there. Good people like Nick Hytner, Richard Eyre and Sam Mendes are all very welcoming and make you feel really relaxed. They know what they want and they know what they want from you. This again is a great way of auditioning. Often you go in and the director says, why don't you try this or why don't you try that. To a certain extent this can be good because they are trying to see how flexible you are. But sometimes it's not about that, it's about them literally not knowing what they want. You want them to know what they want from you; to take care of you for the next five to twenty minutes. And for nothing they ask of you to be a waste of your time.

I remember auditioning for *Martin Guerre* in the West End. I didn't mind auditioning for it, but I had to audition four times. I'd already worked with Declan Donnellan and the producer Cameron Mackintosh, who knew my work from the West End. Perhaps there were a few other people who didn't really know me but, by the third audition, I'd auditioned for everybody. And what is the point of three, four, even five auditions? Sometimes you hear that people have been for fifteen auditions! Maybe I'm missing something but, as an auditionee, I just got to the point where it felt really frustrating. I was doing the same number over and over again. Nobody said they were looking for something that I was or wasn't giving them. I could understand if they didn't want me for the part, but I couldn't understand what they were hoping to achieve after four times of doing the same thing.

It got to the point where I said to my agent I don't want to go in again. I was losing my belief in myself as a performer – not because I didn't get the part, but because I was going in again and again and doing the same thing. I couldn't see what they were gaining from it – they weren't even asking me for a different interpretation.

I think that auditioning can be one of the most demeaning things that you ever have to do, because it is about saying "Am I good enough?" And nobody wants that – we all want to say "I am good enough." But auditioning is the only process by which people can find performers for their work. So you can either walk in with the attitude of "I don't want to do this," or you can go in and say: "This is me, and if you don't think I am right then that is no reflection on me as a person." Then just get on with it because there is no other way around it. And then become so famous that you never have to audition again.

DOMINIC MARSH

Dominic Marsh trained at the Royal Academy of Music. He has primarily worked in theatre, where his credits include: A Midsummer Night's Dream, The Taming of the Shrew, Cymbeline, Twelfth Night, Romeo and Juliet, As you Like It, Oh! What a Lovely War, HMS Pinafore *(Regent's Park Theatre)*, Longitude *(Greenwich Theatre)*, Cinderella *(Oxford Playhouse)*, The Shell Seekers *(UK Tour)*, Hay Fever *(Basingstoke Haymarket)*, Dracula *(Derby Playhouse)*, Racing Demon trilogy *(Birmingham Rep)*, The Lion, the Witch and the Wardrobe *and* Alice in Wonderland *(RSC)*.

I finished the musical-theatre course at the Royal Academy of Music in 2001, so I've been working for five years now. I'd read drama and music at university and then I had a year out before I went on to do my postgraduate year at the Academy. Since graduating I've been fortunate enough to work both in plays and in musicals. Being an actor who sings provides further opportunities for work and increases the variety in my career.

I come from a family of musicians. As a teenager, I loved musicals; at that stage, I didn't particularly enjoy Shakespeare. Now I love working on Shakespeare texts. Interestingly, working on Shakespeare has one major thing in common with working on a song: you have constantly to think on the line. The actors I admire the most are those with the spontaneity and skill to do this.

When I get a musical-theatre audition, the first thing I do is choose my songs. I choose material that suits the character I am auditioning for and I make a real effort to choose pieces that I know very, very well. Then I don't have to worry about words or pitch or whether or not my voice can do it – I can concentrate during the audition on being flexible and taking direction. You've got to choose your pieces well and have confidence in them. It's pointless going in with something you don't quite know.

Having established what I need to take to the audition, I work hard to minimise anything that could cause stress on the day. Never, never be late – it throws you and you don't do your best. But don't get there too early, either. You don't want to be surrounded by other people's tension because that makes you tense.

Recently, I went to an audition and they were running late. There was a verbose actor waiting with the rest of us in the green-room. He couldn't stop talking. Of course, I knew that he was nervous and this was his way of trying to deal with it, but it was really beginning to rattle me. I could feel my own stress level rising. So I went for a walk to the other side of the building and took some deep breaths. You have to do whatever is best for you.

The most important moment of any audition is when the director gives you direction. You have to show a willingness to listen to the director and an ability to act on any suggestions the director makes. They are looking for versatility. When I started, I think I was a bit less willing to be flexible. I just wanted to show what I could do. Now I listen – I really try to concentrate on what they are saying and to give them what they want. It's important to develop a thick skin. Criticism is part of the job. Focus your energy on the positives, not the negatives.

It's important to keep your voice active between jobs. Actors frequently can't afford to have regular lessons, but you can still schedule a time to work on your singing. Don't make excuses – book an appointment with yourself in your diary.

VIVIEN CARE

Vivien Care trained at the Royal Welsh College of Music and Drama and the Royal Academy of Music. She has appeared in The Boy Friend *(Regent's Park Open Air Theatre),* High Society *(Shaftesbury Theatre and Regent's Park),* HMS Pinafore *(Regent's Park),* Les Misérables *(Palace Theatre, Queen's Theatre, the Scandinavian tour and Windsor Castle in the presence of Her Majesty The Queen) and* The Mikado *(D'Oyly Carte at the Savoy).*

Before doing the postgraduate musical-theatre course at the Royal Academy of Music, I trained classically at the Royal Welsh College of Music and Drama. My first job was with the D'Oyly Carte at the Savoy Theatre. I was on stage, seven weeks after I graduated, in the ensemble of the *Mikado*. I'm sure I was the most unconvincing twelve-year-old Japanese schoolgirl the world has ever seen, but I was very, very happy.

I've been in and out of *Les Misérables* a couple of times. I started in the ensemble, then was asked to cover Madame Thénardier. And I did *High Society* at Regent's Park a couple of years ago. Then they went off to do a UK tour, but *Les Mis* had just asked me to come in for a year and I wanted to stay in town. Then *High Society* came into the West End and there was a cast change: I got a call to ask if I would come in as an understudy. That means that you're in the ensemble. So I started rehearsals on Monday and I was on stage for the Saturday matinee. There were five new dance numbers that I'd never even seen before and 15 hours of rehearsal – that's why you have to go to dance classes! You have to keep it up, because you never know what's around the corner.

When I get the call for an audition, everything else stops. I cancel my social life and make sure I get enough sleep. I close down everything and really, really focus on the work. I really look after myself and try to keep myself quiet. Inevitably it never quite happens: life goes on. But it's important to try.

The first thing that I do is to phone one of the singing teachers I see regularly to book an appointment. Even if you think you're in good shape, it's important to see someone who knows your voice, who can help get you up to your playing weight. I go through my music and make sure that I choose appropriate repertoire – at least two songs. I've learned that preparation is the key. This means practising regularly, otherwise you lose your muscle tone – and singing is a muscular activity.

I also spend a great deal of time choosing what to wear: I think it's important. For example, if you're going for *Grease*, polka dots and pedal pushers would be okay. But if you're going for *The Sound of Music*, you might want to be a little more conservative.

Also, it's not enough to come out of college and think, "That's it. I'm ready." I know it's a cliché, but you are only ever as good as your last job and you have to keep re-presenting yourself. And you need to be ever ready, because no one is going to give you a chance to come back again and do it right. It's a one-shot deal.

I had a bad experience that taught me a lot. It was for *Jerry Springer: The Opera*. I really wanted that job: they'd seen me quite a few times already, both for the production in Edinburgh and for the London cast. That's another thing. Recalls don't necessarily bring you any closer. So I suddenly decided I was going to give them a big soprano song, and sang *Climb Every Mountain*. It wasn't even the song I'd worked on with my coach, I just suddenly decided on it. Halfway through I'm thinking, what on earth am I singing this for? At the end of the song I start to attempt this heavy sound. My voice gave out – I couldn't even sing the note. So they asked me, "Would you like to try again?" Once you hear that, you know you're sunk. So I tried it again and my voice just couldn't do it.

It is really important to sing something you know inside out and back to front. Sing something you can sing. Also, when you're waiting to go in, don't chatter away. I try to sit quietly and keep my own counsel. The temptation is to want to be friends with everyone. Don't – there is time enough for that later.

What I've also realised is that it's not always a question of whether or not you're good – it's whether or not you're right. Once you know that, it releases you. You just do what you can. There are no guarantees. But that's okay.

ELIZA LUMLEY

Eliza Lumley trained at the Royal Academy of Music in London. She has performed both theatre and musical theatre; her credits include Ali in the original cast of Mamma Mia!, *Mrs Banks in the West-End production of* Mary Poppins, *Nerissa in* The Merchant of Venice *(for the Royal Shakespeare Company), and The Secretary in* Jumpers *in the West End and on Broadway.*

I've been working for eight or nine years now and I've been lucky in being able to combine straight theatre with musical theatre. I read theology and philosophy at Cambridge University then went to the Royal Academy of Music for two years

I was lucky enough to create the role of Ally in *Mamma Mia!*, then did *The Merchant of Venice* at the RSC. I went to the National for *The Duchess of Malfi* and then did Tom Stoppard's *Jumpers* with Simon Russell Beale which we took to Broadway for five months.

When I'm told I've got an audition, the first thing that I do is get as much information about it as possible from my agent: information about everything that I can – the director, the casting director, the character, the production. Everything.

Then I think about what I'm going to wear. For example, I went out and bought a long straight skirt for Mrs Banks in *Mary Poppins*. I wouldn't go overboard and dress completely as the character – that would feel a bit silly. But the skirt definitely suggested the Edwardian period.

Musical-theatre auditions are much more challenging than straight theatre auditions, where frequently all you have to do is turn up. I go to my book of repertoire and draw up a shortlist. I try not to learn anything new unless it's an audition I don't really care about: after all, you have to try out new material in an audition situation sometime.

Over the years I've learned to try and take control of what is often an out-of-control situation. Now, I only offer songs I want to sing. When I started, I used to offer my whole book and say, "What would you like?" More often than not, they would choose my least favourite song. So, I minimise the choice but cover all the bases. It's important to be really comfortable with your material.

When I'm sent material from the show, I learn it as completely as I can. Then I can forget about the part and start being creative.

I like recalls. I like it when I get to the point that the panel aren't total strangers. I am more relaxed and feel that I can be more creative in the audition. I can let them see more of me. By the time I got to the last audition for *Mary Poppins*, I met Cameron Mackintosh in his living room with a piano. It felt so good. I had got to know the team well at that point and they were bringing me to meet their boss. Everyone was rooting for me.

My seventh audition for *Mamma Mia!* was on a Sunday. I turned up and the door to the audition room was locked. So we ended up driving around London in a taxi with David

Grindrod doing his best to find an audition space while I was chatting to Björn Ulvaeus from *Abba* about my Swedish grandmother. We found a piano and they got me to sing for precisely one minute before I got the job.

What I've learned is to prepare and prepare. Then I really try to enjoy the audition. I really try not to care too much. You've got to do your thing and if you're not right, you've got to learn that it doesn't mean you're not good.

Panels are fascinating. I've sat on some panels: sitting behind that desk, you really want the person who walks through that door to be good. It's when people are too nervous, or haven't prepared properly: that's what stops them from being amazing.

HADLEY FRASER

Hadley Fraser trained at the Royal Academy of Music. He has appeared as Marius in Les Misérables, *Frederick in* The Pirates of Penzance, *Seymour in* Little Shop of Horrors, *John Wilkes Booth in* Assassins, *Kayama Yesaemon in* Pacific Overtures *and Tiernan in* The Pirate Queen *on Broadway.*

I took an English degree at the University of Birmingham and had been doing a bit of acting and singing, so I thought that I'd give musical theatre a go, rather than twenty years down the line regret not having done it. I went to the Royal Academy of Music to do the musical-theatre course and while I was there I auditioned for *My Fair Lady*. I didn't get the job but they remembered me and I got a call from *Les Misérables*, as a result of which I had to leave the Academy two weeks early to play Marius.

Since then, I haven't looked back, really. I did *Pirates of Penzance* at the Savoy Theatre, *The Far Pavilions*, *The Shaughraun* at the Abbey Theatre in Dublin, *Assassins* at the Sheffield Crucible and *The Pirate Queen* on Broadway.

I like to take new material into an audition. When the call comes, I think very hard about what I want to do. I try and tailor songs to each particular job, which keeps me really fresh. If I do something I know too well, I'm not necessarily at my most instinctive, acting-wise. Of course, the danger is you might forget something. But the way I look at it is, they're not there to test your words. I'm not too bothered about losing a line. And if I do, I just stop and ask if I can begin again. This also means I'm constantly extending my repertoire, though I also take along songs I know well. That way, if the panel wants to hear me sing something else, we have a choice.

I'm also careful to do a gentle warm-up before an audition. I make sure that I haven't sung for hours and hours beforehand. For me, it's important not to tire out the voice. After all, when you're in there, they might want you to go through it a few times and you need to have something in reserve.

For a while, I was getting feedback from auditions that they liked my singing voice but felt my speaking voice was weak by comparison. So I've worked hard to centre and ground the speaking voice. Other than that, I haven't changed much vocally in my approach. But what I have learned is that the voice is hugely adaptable and trainable.

My role in *The Far Pavilions* was basically a rock tenor role, quite high up in my register. Then I played John Wilkes in *Assassins*, which is really for bass-baritone. I was quite nervous in case I couldn't manage it, but it was fine. I worked on grounding the voice and lowering my larynx and playing with different textures and timbres. I'm very lucky that I've been given the opportunity to do such different things.

I've learned that you are either exactly the person the audition panel wants, or you're not. And you can't take it any more personally than that. If I really, really want a job, then it's best to try not to psych myself up too much. You can work yourself up to a fever pitch and frequently it's to the detriment of the audition.

The worst experience I had was when somebody very famous, who I was desperate to meet and who shall remain nameless, talked all the way through my audition. Preposterous really, when you've put all that work in. Still, you can't take it personally. The best experience I had was when I'd lost my voice and I didn't think I had a hope – and yet I got the job.

What I've learned is that the panel really is on your side. It's not this Board of Governors which wants to dismiss you out of hand. They want you to be good. You have to hold on to that.

Credits